THE BIG BANG THEORY A-Z

THE BIG BANG THEORY A-Z

AMY RICKMAN

JOHN BLAKE

Published by John Blake Publishing Ltd,
3 Bramber Court, 2 Bramber Road,
London W14 9PB, England

www.johnblakepublishing.co.uk

www.facebook.com/Johnblakepub facebook
twitter.com/johnblakepub twitter

First published in paperback in 2011

ISBN: 978-1-84358-541-1

British Library Cataloguing-in-Publication Data:

A catalogue record for this book is available from the British Library.

Design by www.envydesign.co.uk

Printed and bound by CPI Group (UK) Ltd, Croydon, CR0 4YY

3 5 7 9 10 8 6 4 2

Papers used by John Blake Publishing are natural, recyclable products made
from wood grown in sustainable forests. The manufacturing processes
conform to the environmental regulations of the country of origin.

Every attempt has been made to contact the relevant
copyright-holders, but some were unobtainable. We would be
grateful if the appropriate people could contact us.

Other books by Amy Rickman

Gleeful! A totall unofficial guide to
the hit TV series *Glee*

Vampire Files: Heartthrobs and Bloodsuckers
Blood Brothers

Big Bang

(Because it... *All started with the Big Bang!*)

It was an unlikely formula. Four socially inept geniuses, most of whose dialogue – written in by a professor of astrophysics – is completely incomprehensible to the actors, let alone to the average viewer, gradually befriend a ditzy, blonde wannabe actress-neighbour who shows them what life is really all about. 'I remember reading about [*The Big*

Bang Theory]…and thinking, "Naah, it'll never fly,'" said one TV critic, Bob 'Mr. Media' Andelman, to co-creator of *The Big Bang Theory* Bill Prady. 'At the time, I thought that *Cavemen*, the exact opposite of your show, actually seemed like a better bet on paper.' It was the thought of all that geeky, complicated science that put most critics, including Andelman, off the idea – so much so that he thought a show about cavemen living in modern day San Diego would be a better bet. Could a show dedicated to science really take off with mainstream viewers?

Clearly, it could! Four years since its first airing, *The Big Bang Theory* is one of the fastest growing comedies around the world. It has reached a whole generation of viewers who really connect with Leonard, Sheldon, Penny and the rest of the gang; viewers who had been crying out for a smart but still hilarious show that spoke their language: the language of geeks.

Chuck Lorre and Bill Prady, the two creators of the show, are no strangers to small screen success. They had previously collaborated on *Dharma and Greg*, and had had separate successes with *Two and a Half Men* (for Chuck) and *Gilmore Girls* (for Bill). They knew they wanted to work together again, though, and so they started throwing ideas around for a new pilot.

'We were discussing two different ideas together,' recalled Chuck, speaking to *Collider* magazine. 'One was about a woman who's pretty much getting her life started at the beginning of adulthood. And Bill was talking about the '80s and the genius computer programmers that he was one of.' They put both of these shows into development, and started working up scripts. Fairly quickly in the writing process, they realised that as individual shows the scripts just weren't working. But they did start to wonder what it would be like if Bill's computer programmers met Chuck's ditzy woman. How would they deal with that situation? Suddenly, a light-bulb went off, and they realised they had all the elements to make a show that might really succeed.

Now that they had their great idea, the normal next step for the pair would be to 'pitch' the show to network. A pitch would involve a one- or two-line snapshot of the idea, a detailed outline of the premise, character sketches and a vision for how the show would play out long term. Then would come the nerve-wracking wait to see if the pitch would be given the go-ahead from the powers that be. But because of Chuck's long-standing relationship with the network, and with his track record for success, he was able to bypass the traditional methods and try a more unconventional approach instead. Bill and Chuck wrote down a few key scenes, hired actors and went to the office of CBS President and Chief Executive Leslie Moonves to perform the script live in front of him. 'It was crazy', Chuck said while telling the story to the audience at PaleyFest. The unconventional approach paid off, and the two got the go ahead to make a pilot episode. Of course, it still wasn't an easy road, and they had to work through two different versions of the show to get there. If you want to read more about the unaired version of the show, jump to 'Original Pilot'.

Aronsohn, Lee

Lee is a true jack-of-all-trades in the television industry, covering everything from writing and producing to directing and writing music. He was the co-executive producer of *The Big Bang Theory* from 2007–2011, and helped bring the show to life alongside Chuck Lorre and Bill Prady. He told the *Lincoln Journal Star* (very modestly) that one of his biggest contributions to the show was deciding on Penny's hometown: 'It was something I threw out, I think,' Lee said. 'We knew she

LEE ARONSOHN, *BIG BANG THEORY* CO-CREATOR

wasn't from Los Angeles. So where is she from? Nebraska. I knew a little bit about Nebraska. So fine.'

Lee knew about Nebraska because he lived for two years (1975–1977) in the state capital, Lincoln. Born on 15 December, 1952, he grew up in New York and attended the University of Colorado. He wasn't immediately sure what he wanted to do with his life, and so he moved out to Lincoln to be with his then girlfriend. A lover and collector of comics, he opened his own comic book store in Lincoln called Trade-a-Tape Comic Center (which probably helped with all the comic book knowledge in *Big Bang*!). When he and his girlfriend split, he sold the store to his co-worker Larry Lorenz, who still runs it now.

Left at a loose end, Lee moved to Los Angeles, with the dream of becoming a stand-up comedian. But it wasn't for stand-up that he was bound; although he clearly had comedic talent, he was encouraged by a friend who was a writer and producer on the sitcom *The Love Boat* to consider writing. '[Writing scripts] is like having a term paper due every day of your life,' said Lee, and at first he wasn't interested. But then he was told 'what they were paying writers on *The Love Boat*, and then I said, "On the other hand …".' Fortunately Lee gave it a try, and ended up on the writing staff of

The Love Boat from 1978 to early 1980. Success writing for other sitcoms, like *Who's the Boss?* and *Murphy Brown* followed.

His association with Chuck Lorre goes back to 1993, when they started working together on a show called *Grace Under Fire*. 'We discovered we worked really well together,' Lee continued to the *Lincoln Journal Star*. 'After a while, we learned what we produced together often was better than what either one of us could produce on their own.' With Chuck, he co-created *Two and a Half Men*, and the show premiered in September 2003. Lee has an extra-special involvement with *Two and a Half Men* as he wrote the catchy theme song, which is sung by the three male leads: 'I have two sons, and we used to march around our house singing, "We are men, we are men, we are manly men. We are men, men, men, men, men,"' Aronsohn told the *Journal Star*. 'So when it came time to talk about a theme song for *Two and a Half Men*, I thought, how about something like that?'

After four years with *Two and a Half Men*, Lee came onboard with Lorre's next big hit, *The Big Bang Theory* in 2007. Now, with two of the most successful sitcoms on TV under his belt, Lee can hardly believe his success: 'It's become my reality. When I stop and think about

THE STARS OF TWO AND A HALF MEN, JON CRYER, ANGUS T JONES AND CHARLIE SHEEN

it…I'm not only an executive producer on *Two and a Half Men*, but I'm an executive producer on *The Big Bang Theory*, so it's a very busy life.'

Asperger's Syndrome

Asperger's syndrome is a form of autism. People who are diagnosed with Asperger's syndrome often have difficulty in judging social situations or participating in social interaction. Some people with Asperger's possess a laser-like focus or a high degree of interest in a particular subject. Several times it has been brought up in the media that Sheldon appears to possess many of the traits associated with Asperger's. *Slate* magazine blatantly asked: 'Is the world ready for an Asperger's sitcom?' and wrote: 'a more subtle theme is that Sheldon – flat-toned, gawky, and rigidly living by byzantine rules and routines – appears to have Asperger's Syndrome.'

It's actually a question that Jim Parsons, who plays Sheldon, brought up with the writers as he was diving into the character. They told him that he didn't have the syndrome, but the more research Jim did, the less he was convinced. The similarities are plain to see for anyone who researches the topic. But then Jim wondered whether Sheldon was just so caught up in his work that he naturally cut the world off: 'I think a lot of this really intellectual work that somebody like Sheldon does, the way his brain works, it's so focused on the intellectual topics at hand that thinking he's autistic is an easy leap for people watching the show to make,' he said to the *AV Club*. 'The way Sheldon goes "Huh?" to a social and emotional situation because he's so focused on what he's doing. His brain is so wrapped up in it.'

Bill Prady explained to *Slate* that when he thinks about Sheldon as a character, he doesn't think about Asperger's: 'I just think of his actions as "Sheldony". Some things feel instinctively correct for his character.'

Auditions

Casting for *The Big Bang Theory* was not an easy task: for one, Chuck and Bill had to find actors who could portray complex characters in a manner that would be accessible to the average television viewer. The task was made especially hard by the fact that the two creators hadn't quite decided on the best direction for the show. In fact, because of this they didn't get the casting quite right in the first instance.

The most crucial casting of the whole show was for the two leading men: geniuses and roommates, Sheldon and Leonard. Their chemistry had to be perfect, plus the actors had to be funny in front of a live audience – not an easy thing to do by any means. Luckily, in Johnny Galecki and Jim Parsons, Chuck and Bill had found the perfect people, right from the start.

Chuck had known Johnny Galecki from his previous work on *Roseanne*. Initially, Johnny came in to read for the part of Sheldon, although he was immediately more drawn to Leonard, the slightly more 'normal' roommate. It didn't take much to convince Chuck that Johnny was right for the role: 'We knew Johnny, and felt his sweet – often self-effacing – nature would be a perfect fit [for Leonard].' Johnny was thrilled to land the part, his first major role since his stint on *Roseanne* ended in 1997.

For Jim Parsons, who would eventually get the part of Sheldon, he didn't know quite what to expect from the auditions. In fact, he was expecting something quite different! 'When my agent called and told me I was reading for the new Chuck Lorre sitcom, I didn't know who that was. I thought it was Chuck Woolery, who hosted *Love Connection*. I thought, "It's weird he's writing a show, but I'll go in!" Thankfully, it was not *Love*

Connection, Part II.' Once he received the script, however, all his reservations fell aside and he fell in love with the character of Sheldon, and the magical cadence of the complex dialogue he had to perform. He knew that if he didn't get the part, he might not ever have the chance to play a character this amazingly well-written again, and so he went in with 100 percent determination. 'I enjoy auditioning,' said Jim Parsons on Backstage TV. 'Maybe you're not interested in the part and maybe you're there for other reasons, but if you are interested in it, you have to go for it. It sometimes helps me to think about it like that…This is the only time I'll have to get to do it, or could be.' Jim went for the role with laser-like focus.

In fact, Jim might just have been too good. Chuck Lorre remembers being absolutely floored by Jim's performance, and he actually couldn't believe that Jim could do it again: 'The first time Jim read for Sheldon I thought he must have gotten lucky, that can't be real, it can't happen again. I said, "Bring him back [into the audition room] and he'll break your heart."' Meanwhile, Bill had more confidence in Jim, 'I said "that's the guy"', and not only did he not break our hearts he did it better. His performance on the second audition, when he locked into it, has never changed. It's weird.'

Once they had decided on Leonard and Sheldon

separately, the true test came when they brought them together. Johnny and Jim first met while waiting nervously outside the audition room. They knew they would be auditioning together, and Johnny asked Jim if he wanted to practice their lines together first. Jim's response was: 'No!' That might've fazed some other actors, but not Johnny, who remembers replying, 'Perfect. I like you already.' And from that very first interaction, they were set. Luckily, even without practice, it all went incredibly smoothly: 'The first time they read together, it was real obvious that we had a remarkable combination of talents, really something,' said Chuck to *Delaware County Magazine.* 'For these two [Jim and Johnny] it was one of the cases of the joys of casting, when somebody walks in and just blows your mind.'

After finding the two main men, they needed to find the right leading lady. This proved to be one of the more difficult casting jobs, as the very first incarnation of show called for a character called 'Katie', a very coarse, sarcastic, sexy girl who was comfortable being quite mean to Leonard and Sheldon. Kaley Cuoco came in to audition for Katie but didn't get it – although that wasn't because she disappointed the show's creators. She was simply not quite right for that character: 'Originally when I went to [audition] for

[*The Big Bang Theory*], Chuck and I fell in love with each other and we had a good connection, but he told me, "Honestly, I think you're a little too young for this role." The part went to Canadian actress Amanda Walsh instead. But the pilot didn't work with Amanda/Katie as the lead, and Chuck and Bill rewrote the character into the Penny we know now: the sweet, affable aspiring actress who was more of a friend to Sheldon and Leonard than a manipulator. 'A year passed and a lot of the script changed, and it ended up being perfect for me,' said Kaley to *TV Guide*. 'It worked out for everybody.'

With the changes in the script came two new characters that needed to be cast: Raj and Howard. Even this proved to be quite a challenge, as most people who came in played up to all the stereotypes they could think of: 'Most of the actors who auditioned were kind of doing what they'd seen,' said Chuck Lorre to *Delco* magazine. 'They were playing the absent-minded professor, or they were doing something they'd seen in film or television as opposed to actually embodying the character.'

For Raj's character, they were looking for a first generation American of 'ethnic' descent; even though the character's scripted last name was Koothrappali, they were open to actors of all ethnicities, not just Indian. In fact, in the original version of the script, Raj's character's first name was Dave! 'When I went in there, I am from New Delhi, so I wanted to bring that side of me,' said Kunal Nayyar, who eventually landed the role. 'I used my original accent that I have and I sort of cultivated it from some of my cousins in India. It worked out and they liked it from the beginning.' In fact, the show's creators changed the character's first name to 'Raj' simply because of 'how Indian' Kunal sounded! It's always a good sign that the writers are happy with an actor, when they are willing to adapt a character to suit them.

Meanwhile, Simon Helberg got a call from his agent about a part on *The Big Bang Theory*. When asked by TV.com whether he would consider himself for a nerdy role, he said: 'I have an agent that judges me like that. I could never put myself into that category. I would take nerd out of that. Suave, handsome, bilingual, trilingual. I did get a call that was along the lines of, "You might be perfect for this ridiculously nerdy guy." And I guess I won't take it personally that I got hired.' Simon's audition went smoothly, and with that he became Howard Wolowitz.

Critics agree that the casting of the show is what has

AMANDA WALSH, WHO PLAYED THE FEMALE LEAD IN THE ORIGINAL
BIG BANG THEORY PILOT EPISODE

made it so strong. Luckily all the current cast aced their auditions, or else it would be very different from what we know now!

Awards

Since it's inception in 2007, *The Big Bang Theory* and its cast have won several big television awards. The stand-out actor has really been Jim Parsons, who plays Sheldon. He was first recognised by the Television Critic Awards in 2009, when he won the Individual Achievement in Comedy award. The show itself won the Outstanding Achievement in Comedy award at the same ceremony, and then followed up with a People's Choice award in 2010.

Yet even bigger accolades were due to come for Jim, and he won the Emmy for Outstanding Lead in a Comedy Series in 2010. 'It's really an honour,' said Jim. 'It just feels like being part of a small part of history. I'm a big reader of almanacs – or I was – and I like lists. Boy, do I sound OCD. So I was oddly thrilled to be part of a list like this. The winning was beyond. I'm thrilled, I'm honored. But I'm stunned too.' He also had the fun experience of being awarded his Golden Globe Award for Best Performance by an Actor in a

Television Series (Musical or Comedy) by his co-star Kaley Cuoco in 2011. She was ecstatic to be able to give the award to him, as a win for Jim feels like a win for the whole cast.

OPPOSITE: JIM PARSONS WITH CO-STARS KALEY CUOCO AND JOHNNY GALECKI

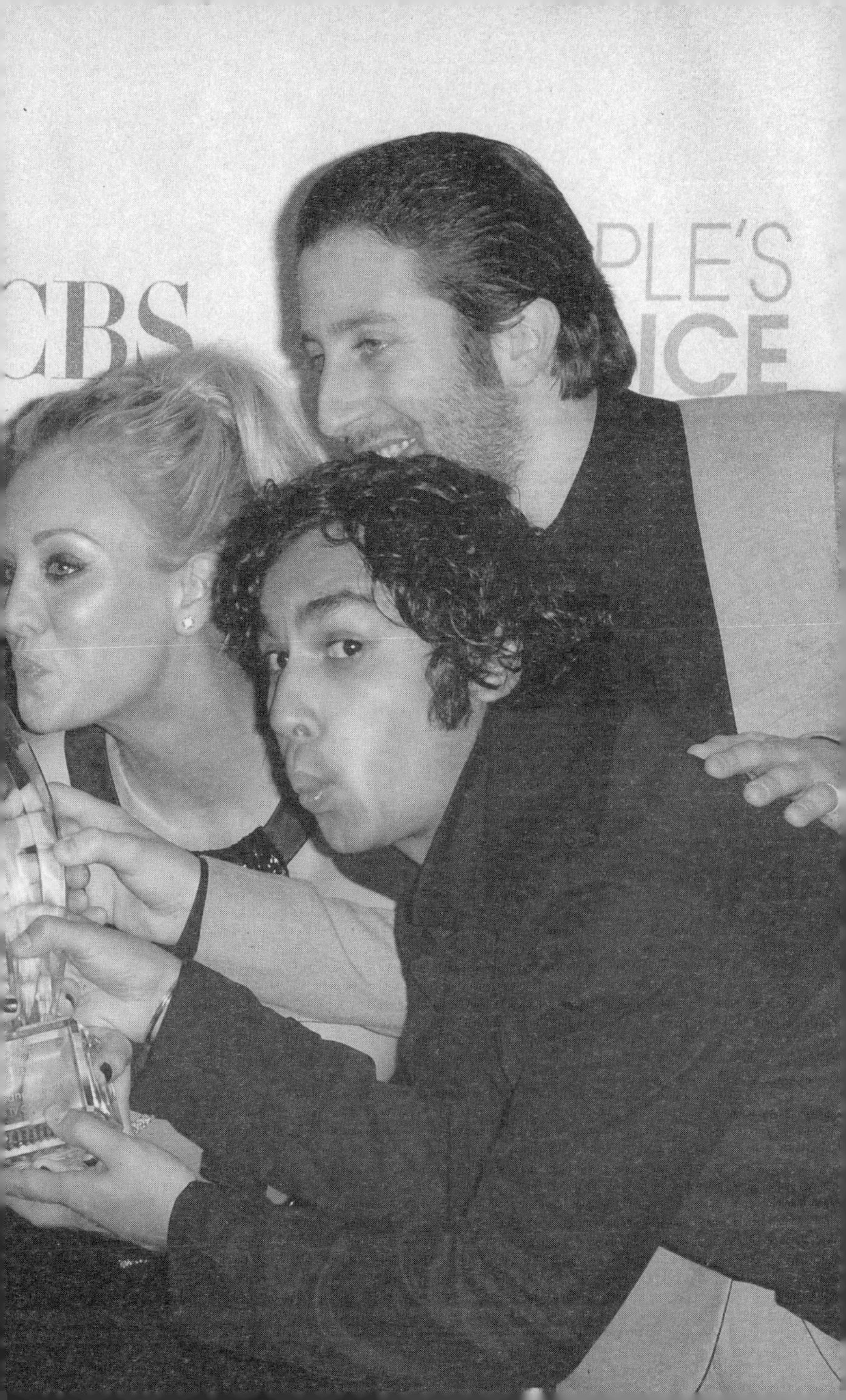
CBS
PLE'S
ICE

B

Barenaked Ladies

Barenaked Ladies are a Canadian alternative rock band and the masterminds behind *The Big Bang Theory* theme song, 'The History of Everything'. The band began in 1988, started by two friends Ed Robertson and Steven Page from Scarborough, Ontario, which is just outside of Toronto. They're best known for their hit single 'One Week', which features their trademark comedy-rap lyrics.

Executives at CBS, the network responsible for *The Big Bang Theory*, initially tried to dissuade Chuck Lorre and Bill Prady from having such an elaborate theme song, thinking that it would cut too much into the running time of each episode. But the creators knew that if anyone could pull off their elaborate musical brief – to condense the entire history of the universe into 32 seconds and make it as iconic as the *Friends* theme tune – it would be the Barenaked Ladies. Simple, right?

The brief came at the perfect time for Ed Robertson, who had coincidentally finished a book on the subject matter: 'I'm a total science geek and I had just read a book by Simon Singh called *Big Bang: Everything You Need to Know about the Most Important Discovery of All Time*,' said Robertson to *Spinner* magazine. 'It's kind of a layman's explanation of every scientific discovery that led up to cosmological theory. So I had just read that and then I got asked, "Would you be interested in writing a theme song for a show called *The Big Bang Theory*?"' It seemed like fate. Immediately, ideas for lyrics and images flooded Robertson's mind and he was really excited to get to work on it. But he had also been burned by the television industry before, and had spent many hours working on a song only to have it be rejected at the last minute. So he double-checked with Chuck and Bill whether anyone else was in the running to write the theme song: 'There was sort of a pause and

they said, "Well, you're the only one we've asked. We really want you to do this,"' he told *News OK*. 'And I said, "Well, that's great because I can give you what you're looking for if you can tell me what you want." So it was a great relationship right from the start.'

'A couple of weeks later he emailed us a guitar vocal demo of that song and it was incredible,' said Chuck in a *Television Without Pity* interview. 'I couldn't believe it. I mean we at one point were saying let's just put the demo on and he goes, "No, no no. I want to put the whole band on and do a whole big production number of this thing"'. Chuck loved the acoustic original though, and would still like to feature it on the show one day. 'We really at some point have to play just the bare bones demo of just him and the guitar, an acoustic guitar. It's terrific. And then the big production number is a whole other animal and now it's the only thing I can imagine being at the top of the show. They just nailed it. All we had to do at that point was just work with them and try and figure out how to edit it so that it could be short enough to air in that tiny window of time at the top of the show.' The theme song has now become an iconic part of every episode, and it would be impossible to imagine the show without it. Ed Robertson said to *News OK* that it has also become a popular element to their live sets now, too: 'We played it one night just kind of on a lark, and people went nuts. It's one of the hits in the set now.'

Bazinga!

'Bazinga!' is Sheldon's trademark saying, which normally follows a prank or joke made by him (his equivalent to using the phrase 'gotcha' or similar). The term was first used in season 2, episode 23, 'The Monopolar Expedition', and has become a cult phrase from the show. It has even found its way into the Urban Dictionary and onto many *Big Bang Theory*-related T-shirts and other merchandise.

Beautiful Mind, A

A Beautiful Mind (2001) features Russell Crowe as the genius Nobel Laureate mathematician John Nash. John Nash was a math prodigy, and won the Nobel Memorial Prize for Economics in 1994 for his work on game theory. He was also a troubled mind, with a documented history of schizophrenia, which the film manifested in both visual and auditory hallucinations. The movie also portrays him as having problems developing social relationships (saying he prefers math to people), which leads Penny to ask whether Sheldon is one of those 'beautiful mind types' in the pilot episode of *The Big Bang Theory*.

Beauty and the Geek

Beauty and the Geek was a reality show dreamed up by *Dude, Where's My Car?* star and *Punked!* creator Ashton Kutcher. Running in the U.S. from 1 June, 2005 to 13 May, 2009, the show paired up eight teams of brainiac or socially awkward guys with a beautiful, popular but shallow girls. Together they teams had to compete to win challenges, with the winning team walking away with $250,000 and hopefully a new perspective on life. *Beauty and the Geek* is considered a precursor to *The Big Bang Theory*'s success, part of the same trend in geek-centric TV that sprung up in the mid-noughties.

Bialik, Mayim

Mayim Bialik had her first mention on *The Big Bang Theory* before she had even heard of the show, and three seasons before she was hired to join the cast. When Sheldon is booted off their team for the physics

Mayim Bialik, who plays Amy Farrah Fowler

bowl for being, well, just plain annoying (Season 1, Episode 13, 'The Bat Jar Conjecture'), Leonard, Howard and Raj attempt to find a fourth member. Before deciding on Leslie Winkle, Raj suggests 'the actress who played TV's *Blossom*'. That just so happens to be Mayim Bialik: child star, neuroscientist and proud mum. 'No, I'd actually never seen the show before I went in to audition. I'd heard I'd been mentioned during the earlier seasons, because of my degree in neuroscience, but I have two little kids so TV time is scarce. I actually thought it was some kind of game show,' she said to Poptimal.

Mayim started acting from the age of eight, in the horror film *Pumpkinhead*. Born on 12 December 1975 in Santa Barbara, California, to a Reform Jewish family, she got her big break when she landed the title role as Blossom Russo in *Blossom*. The show ran for five seasons, from 1990–1995, and established Mayim as one of the defining teenage icons of the nineties.

After *Blossom* ended, however, Mayim didn't continue to act. She knew perfectly well that starring in a sitcom (even in the title role) didn't necessarily mean she was set up to act for life, and she was well aware that many child actresses go off the rails as they get older. So, she decided to go to college: 'I think a lot of it was due to my traditional immigrant background that mandated you go to college and that's just what you do, even if you have your own television show!' she told the *Jewish Press*. She graduated with a Bachelor's degree in Neuroscience, Hebrew and Jewish Studies from UCLA, before joining the PhD program in Neuroscience, which she completed in 2008.

Meanwhile, the acting world was calling her again, and she started to head out for auditions, including one for *The Big Bang Theory*. Chuck Lorre and Bill Prady were searching for a female Jim Parsons – a foil to the fabulous Sheldon, who could grow into a possible love interest for him. When she heard about the role, Mayim Googled Jim and watched some of his scenes – and was impressed by what she saw. 'It's really cool. Originally when they wrote the part, I don't think they knew what kind of scientist she was, but when they found out I was a real neuroscientist, they made her a neurobiologist. I just always loved science.' She aced the audition and was cast as Amy Farrah Fowler. Her first appearance was on the final episode of the season three, and by the middle of season four she was part of the main cast.

As if her acting and academic credentials aren't enough, Mayim is set to become an author as well. Since having her two sons, Miles and Frederick, she has become a spokeswoman for holistic parenting, which advocates breastfeeding, co-sleeping, veganism and green living. She has a book due out in 2012 called *Intuitive Parenting*. For now, she is enjoying the challenge of bringing Amy to life as the season progresses. 'I tell people, I am a neuroscientist, and I play one on TV,' says Dr. Bialik. That's not a boast that many people can make, that's for sure!

Big Bang Theory

So what is the inspiration behind the title? The 'Big Bang Theory' itself is the prevailing accepted theory on how our universe began. It purports that approximately 13.7 billion years ago, the universe began from a single atomic nucleus (known as 'singularity'), before which point no matter existed. This extremely hot, dense state began expanding at a rapid rate that still continues today, and as it expands it cools into the matter that makes up the universe and galaxies as we know them now. The term 'Big Bang' is accredited to Fred Hoyle, who used the term in a radio broadcast in 1949.

Bowie, John Ross

John Ross Bowie plays Barry Kripke in *The Big Bang Theory*. Born on 30 May, 1971 in New York City, New York, John is an experienced comedian, and is a regular performer with sketch comedy group the Upright Citizens Brigade Theater, in both New York and Los Angeles. Apart from *The Big Bang Theory*, he has also been featured on *Glee* and in the film *What the Bleep Do We Know*.

Broken Legs and Bad Driving

Kaley Cuoco (Penny) is one accident-prone actress! On 13 September 2010, Kaley experienced a horrific horse-riding accident that kept her out of work for two episodes in Season 4. She was at one of her regular horse-riding lessons, practicing her jumps and improving her form, 'and at the end of the lesson my horse spooked,' she told Ellen on the *Ellen DeGeneres Show*. 'I wasn't really expecting it and I fell off. I fell off and I was laughing and my trainer was laughing, it was really very silly. So I was getting up and my horse was still kind of spooking. He was in the corner, trying to get away from me. He leapt over me and landed on my leg.'

The impact shattered her leg, turning her foot almost all the way around. 'I went to pick it up, because I was just super-shocked. So I picked it up and the whole thing just came down. It was just dangling. It was horrendous…When they finally cut the boot off, it was open and all the bones were sticking out. It was really bad.' Kaley was rushed to the hospital, and the doctors were not optimistic about her chances. They even warned her that they might have to amputate her foot if it turned out that she had contracted an infection. There was a good chance that Kaley might never have been able to walk again. Like the true comedian she is, Kaley tried to look at the funny side of things, even though she knew how traumatic that outcome would be: 'All I'm thinking is, I'm going to have to call work and tell them I have one foot! That's all I was thinking.'

Two surgeries with the best doctor at Cedar's Hospital in LA, three metal bars and thankfully two feet later, Kaley was released from the hospital, with an extremely positive diagnosis and an expectation of a full recovery. She ended up being written out of only two episodes in Season 4, which did not cause the show too many problems. Kaley even came to the taping that she missed out on, and thanked all the writers for being patient with her, and to apologize for giving them such

KALEY CUOCO, WHO HAS HAD HER FAIR SHARE OF ACCIDENTS IN RECENT YEARS!

a scare. 'I realised, at that moment, that I never wanted to be away from there again. Even now, I cry at every curtain call, because my leg was so badly affected that they didn't know if I would walk again. I am severely, severely grateful.' Only six months later, and she was feeling almost 100% better: 'I'm feeling great. I was at the gym the other day and I cannot remember what leg it is, that's how good I'm feeling. About a month or two ago it took a turn for the better, and I've had no issues. I'm very grateful,' she said to TVline.com

It's not the first time that Kaley has given people a scare, however. She is especially prone to getting into accidents involving motor vehicles, big and small. Once, on holiday in the Dominican Republic, she put her co-star Johnny Galecki's (Leonard) life in real danger. She was driving a Vespa (a motorised scooter), with Johnny hanging on for dear life on the back: 'I ran us right into the wall, and he went flying. I almost killed Johnny Galecki. I'm dead serious,' she recalled to *Maxim* magazine. She then added: 'I've had so many [driving accidents], I can't even count.' Her bad driving with all kind of motorised vehicles is a running joke with the cast. At Comic-Con in 2008, one of the panel members revealed that the cast had rented a boat to explore the California coastline, to which Chuck Lorre replied, 'Let me get this straight, my entire cast was on a boat with Kaley driving in the middle of the ocean?!' Kaley has to be careful, as the show is due to continue for many years, and we would like all the co-stars to be there with it!

C

Caltech University

Sheldon, Leonard, Raj and Howard all work at Caltech University in Pasadena, California, pursuing their various fields of research. Caltech (or the California Institute of Technology) is a private research university founded in 1891, and is regarded as one of the most prestigious universities for science and engineering in the United States. It has 31 Nobel Laureates amongst its alumni and faculty, giving it the highest ratio of alumni-to-Nobel-prize-winners of any other university in the world. No wonder Sheldon Cooper is on the staff there, as statistically he has the best chance of achieving his ultimate goal of winning a Nobel Prize! *The Big Bang Theory* isn't the only show to establish the intelligence of its characters by using Caltech as a base: *Numb3rs*, a show about a genius mathematics professor who uses maths to solve federal crimes is sometimes filmed there (although they call the university by a fictional name, the California Institute of Science).

Canuck Love

Despite starting off slowly, as of early 2011 *The Big Bang Theory* is the most-watched television show in Canada, with an audience that regularly tops three million viewers – more than *American Idol* and *Dancing with the Stars*, its two closest rivals. It airs on the channel CTV. '[The Canadian fans] have been amazing,' said Kunal Nayyar (Raj). 'I didn't know the show was so big here, it's a lovely feeling.'

If that wasn't enough, the Royal Canadian Institute for the Advancement of Science announced that they were giving honorary membership to co-creators Chuck Lorre and Bill Prady: 'We are honouring Chuck Lorre, Bill Prady and the entire *Big Bang Theory* team for creating a television program that seamlessly melds science and everyday life,' said Bruce Gitelman, President, RCI. 'The program exposes the public in an entertaining way to the awe and wonder of science and life in general. As the number one series in Canada today, it not only makes science accessible to the public but also entertains many practicing scientists.' Canada is hooked on *The Big Bang*, that's for sure!

Cheesecake Factory, The

The Cheesecake Factory is a restaurant in Pasadena, California, where Penny works. There is a real Cheesecake Factory in Pasadena, CA, part of a chain of family friendly restaurants that are located throughout the U.S. However, *The Big Bang Theory* does not shoot on location at the restaurant; rather, they film on a set that bears little resemblance to a real Cheesecake Factory. The interior design isn't the only thing that's different, however: 'I think *The Big Bang Theory*'s version of the Cheesecake Factory uniform is a little different. Just a little!' said Kaley Cuoco to TV Guide online. In the real restaurants, Cheesecake Factory waiters and waitresses wear an all-white uniform, as opposed to Penny's white shirt, mustard vest, green apron and blue skirt combination.

Kaley Cuoco's character, Penny, works at the Cheesecake Factory in the show

That doesn't mean that the Cheesecake Factory doesn't appreciate the free plug, though! Kaley gets special treatment whenever she goes into the restaurant. She told *Delaware Country* magazine: 'I went into the Cheesecake Factory a couple of times recently, and I'm always, like, "Why is everyone looking at me?" And they are saying, "Do you know anything about the Cheesecake Factory? We love you. We love you." And I always forget that my character works there. They always give me funny looks, but it's very cute.'

Comic-Con

Comic-Con is short for the annual four-day Comic-Con International: San Diego, which highlights science fiction and fantasy, comic books and popular media. It is the largest convention in North America. In recent years, it has become a frequent test-zone for previewing material to audiences, especially for television shows or movies that have some kind 'geek cred', which would've made *The Big Bang Theory* a perfect choice.

Yet *The Big Bang Theory* didn't launch there, as Chuck and Bill had no idea how big the show was going to be. Rather, the cast and crew had their first Comic-Con experience after one season of the show had already aired on television, in summer of 2008. They had no idea what to expect, and Johnny Galecki (Leonard) was afraid they wouldn't be well-received: 'I thought it was a terrible idea, that the collectors and fans would think it was offensive that this nerd show was visiting,' said Galecki to *Stepping Out* magazine, 'but it was the exact opposite.'

In fact, to hear Chuck talk of it, the cast and crew were all amazed. 'It was exhilarating,' said Chuck Lorre to Television Without Pity. 'I had never been to Comic-Con before and I wasn't really sure if we belonged there. And our reception was, it was, I dunno…I was stunned. I was hoping for a few hundred people in a small room. But what was it? Was it a couple of thousand people?' A couple of thousand people meant standing room only for the avid fans in the room, and the panel was bombarded with insightful questions by a clearly knowledgeable audience who were well-versed about the show and the characters – and who clearly loved it. It was the first time that the cast and crew realised just how big the show really was.

Exploring Comic-Con was also a useful experience for the writers especially, as it helped them get to grips with what was popular with their target audience: the nerds. 'What I took away most from [Comic-Con] was the whole atmosphere of it was a celebration of what people love,' said Chuck. 'And the costumes and all that stuff is just an aspect of that celebration. I just thought the energy there was terrific. We walked around. Just wandered around the convention floor and it was just fun. The whole experience was wonderful.' They loved it so much, Chuck wondered if they could write a visit Comic-Con for the gang into the series itself. 'We would have loved to have done something with Comic-Con. We just didn't have the time. We would have loved to come down here and shoot some scenes down here. How exciting would that be?' Bill Prady even took to thinking about what costumes Sheldon and Leonard would wear to the convention. After already seeing them in costumes as varied as the Doppler Effect, Frodo Baggins and, of course, the Flash, it seems like the characters have plenty of costumes to choose from! 'There would be an argument because Leonard would say "Let's all pick our own costumes," and Sheldon would want some sort of group theme,' said Bill to *Collider*. 'He would want it "we're all either from the same film" or "we all represent the same idea" like different *Star Trek* uniforms from different shows or "we're all villains from different things". His compulsion for order and arrangement and his need to impose that on the group would be problem number one for picking costumes for Comic-Con.' There would be many problems with the show being at Comic-Con, however, as there are copyrighted logos everywhere, which the show would be prohibited from filming.

Chuck Lorre summed up exactly how they felt after they left the convention floor in 2008: 'We left San Diego three feet off the ground. Everybody in the cast. It was a heartwarming experience to see that the show had meant something to people. It was as meaningful to the people watching it as it is to us. That was terrific.' The cast have been back every year since then, delighting fans with their warm personalities and funny, insightful panels.

Cooper, Leon N

Leon N Cooper won the Nobel Prize for Physics in 1972, which he was awarded for his contribution to the theory of superconductivity, often called the BCS-theory. He is the inspiration for Sheldon's last name.

Cooper, Sheldon Lee

Dr. Sheldon Cooper, B.Sc., M.Sc., M.A., PhD, Sc.D., is a 29-year-old theoretical physicist working at Caltech

University. His work is mostly focused on proving string theory, which he is working hard to credit over loop quantum gravity. He lives with his flatmate and best friend Leonard Hofstadter in apartment 4A of their building in Pasadena, California. Known for being 100 percent unapologetic about his intelligence, he often misreads social cues, adheres to a strict routine, has an eidetic memory and struggles to understand sarcasm. He was born in Galveston, Texas, into a strongly Evangelical Christian family headed up by his dad, George, and mum, Mary and has two siblings – older brother, George Cooper Jr. and his twin, Missy. He is often called 'Shelly' by his family, and is known as 'Moonpie' to his grandmother (whom he calls 'Meemaw').

The character of Sheldon is based on the computer programmers that Bill Prady knew back in the 1980s. 'I would tell Chuck [Lorre] about a guy I knew who was a human calculator. If you programmed in Z80 assembly you had to convert from decimal to hexadecimal and you could either grab the calculator or you could shout it to this guy and he would be faster. But he couldn't calculate a tip at a restaurant. And the reason is because the formula for a tip is 15–20% depending upon the quality of the service and he couldn't put a numeric value on the service. It was human,' said Bill. Yet some of Sheldon's traits are taken from Bill himself: 'Chuck, who's known me for eleven years, has gently tried to tell me that when we go up a flight of stairs, it's not important that I always teach him the thing about the difference in tread height and how a difference of only two millimetres…will cause most people to trip,' laughed Bill to *Deseret News*. This exact scene appeared in the pilot episode of *The Big Bang Theory*.

Sheldon is currently linked to Amy Farrah Fowler, but whether the pair can be defined as 'in a relationship' is still debatable.

Sheldon is played by award-winning actor Jim Parsons. 'Jim embodies the role,' praises Chuck Lorre. 'You can't teach that. The way he walks, the way he sits, the way he holds his kitchen utensils. He even listens as Sheldon.'

Cricket vs. Baseball

One side effect of having such a multinational cast is that there are some heated sports-related debates! Kunal Nayyar (Raj) is a huge fan of cricket, and tries to get the other cast members involved, to little success! 'They don't get it, obviously,' said Kunal. 'You know, except for

Jim [Parsons], no one else is a big sports fan.' Instead, Jim and Kunal debate about which sport is 'slower' – cricket or baseball!

For, Kunal cricket is a lifelong passion: 'I grew up like any other kid in Delhi playing cricket since I was five or six years old. I went to cricket camp in the summer. I played a lot of cricket for fun and at school. I was never really great, but I was a huge cricket fanatic. For me, getting on the field was a dream. Anytime we had a moment, we'd go into our driveway with a tennis ball and cricket bat and play,' he said to imbatman.org.

If Kunal was going to arrange a cricket tournament with the cast, he'd have a tough time putting a team together – none of them are particularly athletic! In fact, he thinks the only person who would be any good is Kaley Cuoco, 'because she played tennis at state when she was young and she's athletically inclined…She's probably the best [choice of player]. The worst? Pick any of the three guys. They're all terrible.'

Crippler, The

It's one thing to write about a fighting robot, and another one to actually watch one in action – at least, that's what happened to Chuck Lorre and Bill Prady when they decided to include one in their show 'It scared the s★★t out of us is what it did!' The fighting robots appeared in Season 2, Episode 12 'The Killer Robot Instability'. In the episode, the boys build a robot to battle against the robot of their greatest enemy, Barry Kripke. Unfortunately for them, Kripke's robot is more than a match for theirs. In real life, too, the Crippler was quite the formidable machine. Bill Prady told IGN how they tested it out: 'They took the prop cart, the rolling cart, and put the [Crippler robot] after it, and it threw it about five feet in the air and just destroyed it. Tore it apart. So yeah, [it was] very cool.'

Critical Reception

When the pilot first aired on 24 September 2007, it was a nervous moment for all involved. How would TV viewers receive it? How would critics rate the show? Yet for one member of the cast, Simon Helberg, those nerves were overshadowed by the dominant feeling that things were going to be okay. The feeling grew as they were working in front of a live audience for the first time. 'There was a distinct moment, in shooting the pilot, when I knew the show would work,' said Simon to *Watch!* magazine. 'I was offstage and heard the audience's reaction, which went on for so long that the director, Jim Burrows, said, "There's too much laughter. We have to go back and do it again." Then, when Kunal [as the girl-shy, Indian-born Rajesh Koothrappali] and I came in, we got entrance applause – and no one knew who we were yet! I just remember thinking, "This is something special."'

Simon might have been especially confident, but the initial critics' reviews were decidedly mixed. 'And I don't fully blame them,' Jim Parsons (Sheldon) admitted to *Watch!* magazine. 'The show is better than its description. But I don't know how to describe it.' One critic from the *Washington Post* was lukewarm about the pilot: 'Laugh-packed though the series pilot is, the show also suffers from a kind of conceptual claustrophobia that could limit its appeal and its life span. Although the funky-clunky pairing of the two characters and the actors who play them is deft, the universe they inhabit is awfully narrow.' The review in *USA Today* brought up similar concerns, and highlighted the same bright spots – the actors in the show. The pilot did just enough to entice the reviewer to stick around for another week: 'Still, here's another of Lorre's habits: His shows tend to get better after the pilot. This may not be the sitcom breakthrough for which we've all been hoping, but Lorre has produced a first episode that leaves you eager to try the second.' Other reviewers, including the influential *LA Times*, wondered if there was much substance to the show beyond the pilot: 'It's just the same joke endlessly repeated – the everyday translated into geek-speak, and the obscure and difficult treated as if it were common knowledge.'

Yet one review in particular summed up most the fear surrounding the show's entire concept. The *Chicago Tribune* reviewer slated the show's pilot episode: 'I'm not sure what Chuck Lorre has against smart people, but with the foul sitcom *The Big Bang Theory* he tries to have his revenge against anyone with an IQ above room temperature.' Some of the cast knew a review like that was coming. 'The critics assumed that *Big Bang* would be about cheap shots at intelligent people,' Galecki explained to *Watch!* magazine. 'And if anything, I think the show defends intelligent people.' And three seasons later, the same *Chicago Tribune* reviewer, Maureen Ryan, gladly ate her words: '*The Big Bang Theory* has definitively won me over. The show, which has made many smart corrections in its three seasons, has evolved into one of the most enjoyable comedies on the air…The characters have become humanised and

KALEY CUOCO
(PENNY)

multidimensional, their relationships are believable and well-sketched, and the one-liners and jokes are consistently funny.' Just goes to show that even the most damning reviews don't have to be a terminal judgment on a show.

Cuoco, Kaley

Kaley Christine Cuoco plays the gorgeous girl-next-door Penny. She adores the role, and can't quite believe her luck when it seemed like audiences really took to her character and to the show as a whole. Able to embody Penny's sweetness without making her appear overly dumb or ditzy, she was perfectly cast by Chuck Lorre and Bill Prady.

Born on 30 November, 1985, in Camarillo, California, Kaley was destined to be a performer – she just hadn't quite chosen her stage yet. By the age of five, Kaley was already modeling and acting, and had her first big job in the TV movie *Quicksand: No Escape* (1992), alongside Donald Sutherland and Tim Matheson, completed when she was just six years old. Acting came easily to her, and she quickly gained a reputation as a talented and easy-to-work-with child. Work came thick and fast then – ads for Barbie, more modeling work and bit-parts in several TV series followed, but young Kaley even worked on some Hollywood blockbusters like *Virtuosity* (1995) with Denzel Washington and *Picture Perfect* (1997) with Jennifer Aniston. That didn't mean, however, that Kaley was immune to rejection either, but she had a positive attitude that helped her deal with any setbacks that she might have encountered along the way: 'I learned rejection so young,' she told *The Examiner*. 'My parents told me that it's not going to be fun all the time. When I was little, I was working a lot and it was great and I was thinking this is the easiest thing ever. Anyone can do this. But then you get older and people say, "You are so not right for this". I was right for everything when I was 6!! I formed a very thick skin at a young age. Even now, even though it's such a great job, it is still to me a job. I do other things. This is not my life.' Being a child actress meant that she didn't really have the 'typical' American high school experience, but she didn't regret a minute of it: 'I had the greatest childhood ever,' she told *Maxim* magazine. 'I was friggin' 10 years old, running around on the set of *Virtuosity* with Denzel Washington, doing whatever the hell I wanted…High school prom? Screw that. I went to cast parties. They were so much better than the prom.'

Yet despite clearly having a talent for acting, Kaley was also passionate about a different type of 'performance': tennis. She started playing tennis when she was three years old, and eventually wound up being a nationally-ranked amateur on the tennis circuit. 'I played since I could walk. I grew up on a tennis court. My whole family played,' she said to *Stepping Out*. She loved the competitiveness of the sport, and saw the 'grunting' of her fellow players on the court as just another type of acting – albeit this time to intimidate their opponent! The court was another stage for her. By the time she was 16 though, she was faced with difficult choice of whether to continue training to become a professional tennis player or dedicating herself to acting full-time. When, in the spring of 2002, she was offered a leading role on television sitcom *Eight Simple Rules…for Dating my Teenage Daughter*, the decision was essentially made for her. She was going to act.

Eight Simple Rules ran from 2002 to 2005 and established Kaley as a sitcom actress to watch (see the *Eight Simple Rules* entry for more about Kaley's role on the show). What also set her apart from many other teenage actresses was her lack of scandal; Kaley seemed to have a much more mature outlook on life and

didn't get involved in the Hollywood party scene. 'I don't do anything stupid in front of people,' she told CBS's *Watch!* magazine. 'I don't show my crotch to cameras when I get out of cars. I don't understand some of these people! I get drunk on my own with my friends – I'm not going to go to the Ivy. I've just grown up in this business. It's work to me. It's not my ticket into fun. I can't tell you the last time I went to a club.' Kaley's idea of a fun night in is, 'in front of the TV with my dog. So embarrassing! My glasses, my iPad, my dog. A glass of wine and whatever leftovers I have in the fridge. It's really sad, actually.' Sad though it might be, it showed Kaley off as the true professional she is.

After the end of *Eight Simple Rules*, she took a turn on the cult TV show *Charmed*, with the possibility of her character, Billie Jenkins, getting a spin-off series, although it never materialised. Kaley was quite glad that her career path didn't lead her towards more serious dramas as opposed to sitcoms. 'Dramas require 18-hour days where you want to kill yourself,' said Kaley to the *New York Post*. 'You can have a life while you work on

Opposite: Kaley Cuoco celebrating her 21st birthday with Amy Davidson, who played her on-screen sister Kerry in *Eight Simple Rules*

a sitcom, and I'm selfish. I love my life, and I like to do other things besides work.' Finally, in early 2007, she landed the role we love her best for today, as Penny on *The Big Bang Theory*.

In between shooting for *The Big Bang Theory*, Cuoco featured in a few hit movies. Her first was a lead role in the comedy-horror *Killer Movie* in 2008, alongside *The Vampire Diaries* hottie Paul Wesley. She also starred in *Hop* (1 April 2011) with James Marsden and is due to be seen in *The Last Ride* (also 2011). She's a busy girl! Yet Kaley always remains grounded, and appreciates the success that *The Big Bang Theory* has brought her: 'I've learned not to take anything for granted, and I don't know how I landed a show that is this successful. That's super-rare, so I'm riding this wave as long as I can. I didn't see this coming. I have no idea where life will take me next.'

Although she gave up tennis, Kaley still tries to remain active. She loves to play table tennis and miniature golf, but by far her favourite hobby is horse-riding. She tested the waters in her early teens, when she was still juggling an active tennis career. When tennis was out of the picture, she dedicated herself completely to riding: 'My mom grew up with horses and when I turned 14, 15, she's like, "Do you want to take a riding lesson?" I thought, "Oh, gross, dirty." She was like, "Okay." And then I did and now I'm the one cleaning those damn stalls out. You can't get me away from the barn now. It shocks even me. Trust me. I don't know what happened to me. No heels at that place,' she told *Crave* online. Despite the fact that she would be involved in a freak riding accident in 2010, she still loves to get out there and ride her horses. In fact, her first concern when she broke her leg was that her screams had terrified her pony. Her love of animals has led to her campaigning for many animal-related charitable causes, including the Humane Society of the United States, Animal Avengers and PETA. In 2008 and 2009 she was named one of the world's sexiest vegetarian celebrities by PETA. After her accident, she and her boyfriend Christopher French (of indie rock band Annie Automatic) recorded a rendition of 'Somewhere Over the Rainbow', with all proceeds going to the Humane Society of the United States.

For now, Kaley can't believe her luck that she has ended up on such a great show, which seems to be giving her such a stable career in a time when nothing in show business seems certain. She finds looking to the future difficult, because her present is so great. 'I would probably love to do another sitcom that was revolved all around me,' she told *Collider*, '[but] I'll probably be on this one for awhile, so maybe by the end of this, I won't want to do that. But, if I ended with this, I would be the happiest person.'

Devoted Fans

With its talented, down-to-earth cast, fantastic writing and an attention-to-detail unsurpassed by any other show, it's no surprise that *The Big Bang Theory* has such attentive and devoted fans. Kaley Cuoco (Penny) is blown away by the love: 'We have a different world of fans,' she told *Maxim* magazine. 'There's something about this show that has brought out a group of people I didn't know existed. It's like nerd geniuses have come out of the closet by the thousands. Let's be honest: Our show is the biggest thing that's happened to physics in, like, a bazillion years. The scientists all have a voice now. When we tape our show, it's like a rock concert.'

For Kaley, it seems like there are only two kinds of people in the world: those who have seen the show and have become avid fans, and those who haven't seen it at all. She loves the dedication that *The Big Bang Theory* inspires; it's unlike anything she's ever experienced before. Kaley also told *Stepping Out* magazine about what happens when she gets stopped in the street: 'The fans know everything about everything. They come up and ask me, "When are Sheldon and Penny going to get together?" They have so many crazy questions. It's just so cute! They remember things that I don't even remember. It's just amazing.'

Yet Kaley is a seasoned professional when it comes to acting; Kunal Nayyar, on the other hand, is getting his first nationwide exposure on television and is slowly learning the restrictions as well as the benefits of celebrity: 'I have to be on Facebook under a fake name, you know. I can't just get onto an airplane and fly anywhere I want to now without considering certain things, like logistics, like security or – you know, I can't just go to Comic-Con on my own, check out the comics.'

KALEY CUOCO SMILING FOR THE CAMERAS BEFORE APPEARING ON
THE LATE SHOW WITH DAVID LETTERMAN

Luckily, he knows it's a small price to pay for being on such a well loved show: 'The good thing is it's just nice to be recognised for your work. And I love our fans. They're so passionate and so respectful and kind and lovely and generous.'

Doppler Effect

One of the most loved episodes of the first season is the Hallowe'en episode (Season 1, Episode 6, 'The Middle-Earth Paradigm') where Sheldon comes dressed as the 'Doppler Effect'. The Doppler Effect itself refers to the perceived change in frequency of a wave (either sound or light) as it passes an observer – the most obvious example is a police siren, which sounds higher pitched as it is approaching an observer than when it is moving further away. This theory has applications as far reaching as radar technology and astronomy, where the Doppler Effect is used to calculate how fast stars and other galaxies are moving away (or toward) the earth. Sheldon represents the Doppler Effect by dressing in a black-and-white striped suit, where the white stripes gradually get larger and further away from each other. Unfortunately for Sheldon, most people thought he was just dressed like a zebra.

Dr. Horrible's Sing-Along Blog

Simon Helberg (Howard Wolowitz) is probably one of the busiest actors of the cast, having worked on numerous projects in the breaks between shooting seasons of *The Big Bang Theory*. One project in particular gave him even more geek cred, and would probably put him in the unique position of being an actor that his character would admire in real life. The project was Joss Whedon's 2008 internet sensation *Dr. Horrible's Sing-Along Blog*. A musical performed in three acts, *Dr. Horrible* was written by Joss and his brothers Jed and Zach, and starred Neil Patrick Harris. *Dr. Horrible* is one of the most successful direct-to-internet productions ever made. Through elaborate musical numbers, it told the story of an aspiring supervillain (Dr. Horrible, Neil Patrick Harris) and his sidekick Moist (*The Big Bang Theory*'s own Simon Helberg) in a fight against Captain Hammer (Nathan Fillion) to woo Penny (Felicia Day). It was Joss Whedon's idea to produce something independently of the networks, who were bogged down in the Writers' Guild of America strike of 2007–2008.

For Simon, it was an experience unlike any other. He had become involved with the production as he knew Jed and Zack Whedon from high school. They asked him if he 'wanted to be apart of this little internet thing during the strike. It was conceived to combat the studio. When there was no work being done, we proved we could actually do something.' It was hugely popular, going on to win a Hugo award and an Emmy for Outstanding Short-format Live-Action Entertainment.

Eight Simple Rules

Kaley Cuoco (Penny) was most famous pre-*Big Bang Theory* for her role as Bridget Hennessy in another TV sitcom – *Eight Simple Rules… for Dating My Teenage Daughter*. Bridget was the beautiful, popular, but very superficial older sister of the Hennessy family, which also included smart-but-sarcastic middle child Kerry and annoying younger brother Rory. Because Bridget and Kerry have started dating boys, their father, Paul (played by John Ritter), is prompted to write a column about his struggles dealing with their teenaged suitors –

KALEY CUOCO WITH *EIGHT SIMPLE RULES* CO-STAR AMY DAVIDSON

hence the title of the show. Their mum, Cate, was played by Katey Sagal.

The show ran for three seasons, from 17 September 2002 to 15 April 2005. It was Kaley's first main role, and she relished her first taste of the limelight. It was also a steep learning curve for the actress who was only just having her acting chops tested for the first time. Combined with achieving the regular teenage milestones – like learning to drive – it was an exciting and challenging time for Kaley: 'I was just starting to drive on *8 Simple Rules* and that whole show was a whole big process for me. I didn't even know what I was doing. I learned so much.' In a strange casting twist, the actress hired to play her younger sister, Amy Davidson, was in fact six years older than Kaley, but her youthful looks and small height (being only five feet tall) meant Amy was more suited to playing a younger character.

The star of the show was John Ritter, who played Paul, and he was already a successful and established comedian and sitcom actor from his time on *Three's Company*. On 11 September 2003, John was on set rehearsing for the second season of *Eight Simple Rules* when tragedy struck – he collapsed and was taken to hospital, and passed away later that evening at the age of 54. The cast and crew, along with the entire entertainment industry and his millions of fans, were thrown into a state of shock and grief. It hit Kaley hard, as John had been like a father figure to her. Her gut reaction was not to continue with the show. 'I was going to quit and I wanted people to quit with me,' she told andPop.com. 'I didn't want to do it myself, but I was ready to go...To me, it was the "John Ritter Show" and that's all that mattered. Without John being here, it just didn't seem right. Finally there was a moment when it just hit me. John wouldn't want me to sit on my butt for the rest of my life feeling sorry for myself or sorry for him. As cheesy as it sounds, he would have wanted us to go on.'

Go on, the show did. It continued with Katey Sagal taking over as the lead actor in the series, and the show dealt with the family dealing with the death of their father, just as the actors themselves dealt with John Ritter's death. Despite this, the show never seemed to capture the same audience without him, and by the end of Season 3, ratings had dropped off to terminally low levels. The series was cancelled before a fourth season could begin.

Elevator

There's a reason why the elevator up to Sheldon and Leonard's apartment has been out of order the whole time *The Big Bang Theory* has been running – and it's more than just evidence of one the gang's experiments gone wrong! There is actually a very practical reason why having a broken elevator works for the show. Bill Prady explained: 'Our broken elevator does two wonderful things for us. First, it eliminates the traditional sitcom L-shaped apartment building hallway, and second, it allows us to do "walk and talk" scenes without having to create a city street or similar set. We're proud of the set, which required we jackhammer a hole in the floor of Stage 25 (to make room for the stairs going down). I can't tell you whether it will ever get fixed, but if it does, I'm sure things won't go well.'

Episodes

So far in the history of *The Big Bang Theory*, there have been 87 episodes in total (through the end of Season 4). The episode titles always start 'The...' followed by two-word phrase summing up the plot but designed to resemble a scientific principle or experiment. The one exception was the pilot, which was simply called 'Pilot'. For example, the title for Season 1, Episode 2 is 'The Big Bran Hypothesis'.

In an unprecedented move for any recent TV sitcom, on 12 January 2011 CBS and Warner Bros. Television announced that they were extending *The Big Bang Theory*'s run for three more years, through 2013-2014. 'It doesn't take a theoretical physicist to see why this show is a BIG part of our comedy future,' said Nina Tassler, the president of CBS Entertainment. 'From ratings to critical acclaim to pop culture buzz, it's struck a chord on all levels. The creative genius of Chuck Lorre and Bill Prady and the on-camera talents of an amazing young ensemble have created a comedy that will entertain viewers for a long time. We're proud to partner with Warner Bros. on another highly successful, long-running comedy.'

The cast heard the news as they were rehearsing. Kaley brought up the news with the cast: 'I said, "Hey, guys. Did we get picked up for three years?" Johnny was like, "Oh, yeah. I heard that." Then, Jim said, "Oh, yeah. I heard that, too." Then we just went on with our day. That's how casual we are at work. Later in the day, we did a big "Cheers!" over it. That just doesn't happen, to know you have a job for three more years. It's very emotional for me.'

Knowing that the show has been guaranteed a television slot for the next three years takes a huge weight off the minds of the cast, and it enables the writers to develop storylines over the long term.

Family Guy

It's common knowledge in Hollywood that you haven't made it big until you've been parodied in an animated television show – whether that's on *The Simpsons* or *Family Guy*, if you haven't been made fun of, you're nobody! *The Big Bang Theory*, and specifically cast-mates Johnny Galecki, Jim Parsons and Kaley Cuoco make it on to *Family Guy*, in an episode called 'Business Guy' (Season 8, Episode 9), when Peter Griffin forces his father-in-law, Carter Pewterschmidt, to host a *The Big Bang Theory* viewing party.

Farrah Fowler, Amy

Amy is introduced in the season finale of Season 3, when Raj and Howard trawl through an internet dating site searching for possible matches for Sheldon. Surprisingly, they seem to find Sheldon's perfect match in Amy, a neurobiologist who has as much disdain for the general human population as Sheldon does. They participate in an off-screen 'relationship' during the break between Season 3 and Season 4, where they get to know each other via the internet.

Amy becomes a series regular in Season 4, and against all odds becomes very good friends with Penny. She is played by Mayim Bialik.

Friends

With the success of *The Big Bang Theory* steadily on the rise, many television critics and pundits have been posing the question: is *The Big Bang Theory* the new *Friends*? *Friends* was one of the most popular sitcoms of all time, following the loves, lives and struggles of six twenty-somethings (Ross, Monica, Rachel, Joey, Chandler and Phoebe) in New York City. It was one of the first true 'ensemble cast' shows, with none of the main stars attempting to take precedence over the other.

The series finale of *Friends*, which aired on 6 May 2004, was the fourth-most-watched series finale after *Seinfeld*, *Cheers*, and *M*A*S*H*, and the most-watched episode of television of the Noughties.

Yet, while *The Big Bang Theory* would certainly never say no to the kind of ratings *Friends* achieved over its ten-year life span, the show's creators are reluctant to draw the comparisons too far. In fact, Chuck Lorre is quite defensive about his characters, citing them as having real lives outside of the sitcom: 'They're not slackers. This is not *Friends*. These are very, very remarkable characters and if we stay true to that then it's quite a joy to be a part of.'

Still, despite Chuck's protestations, it is hard not to see the similarities: the main characters live in apartments across the hall from each other; Leonard and Penny have an on-again, off-again relationship analogous to that of Ross and Rachel; both shows have a catchy, transcendent theme song. Bill Prady, on the other hand, is flattered by the comparison, and respects what *Friends* did for the sitcom genre as a whole. He is happy to try to pick up tips from their success: 'I think that [*Friends*] succeeded by having respect for its characters by believing in its characters as real people,' said Bill to Bob Andelman (aka Mr. Media). It's this consistency of character that Bill and Chuck try to emulate when writing for the show. 'I think shows that fail often fail because the characters change,' continued Bill. 'One of the things that we have here is an almost obsessive need to protect who these characters are, not to say well, this is a funny joke, let's use it if it flies in the face of who these characters are and what they would really do.' The challenge for the writers of *The Big Bang Theory*, however, is that their characters are not instantly relatable – whereas most people could immediately sympathise with Rachel starting out on her own as a waitress, or with Chandler's tedious office work, theoretical physics isn't exactly the most accessible career. Still, there's a universality of emotion that Chuck and Bill try to tap into, in the same manner as *Friends*: 'You can't relate to the notion of presenting a paper at a conference on physics, but you can relate emotionally to an argument with somebody you've done work with as to how you should proceed, as to how partners should proceed in something. So that's the goal: to create an emotional connection.'

Galecki, Johnny

John Mark 'Johnny' Galecki plays the loveable, geeky experimental physicist Leonard, who is often painfully aware of his own social awkwardness. In real life, Johnny has no such problems, and has managed to maintain a successful acting career since his early twenties.

Johnny was born in Bree, Belgium on 30 April 1975. His dad, Richard Galecki, was stationed in Belgium as part of the U.S. Air Force and his mum, Mary Lou, worked as a mortgage consultant. He has two younger siblings, Nick and Allison. When Johnny was three years

Johnny Galecki, who plays Leonard Hofstadter

old, the family moved to Oak Park, Illinois, just outside of Chicago, and his father got a job rehabilitating veterans in a local hospital.

Johnny was a precocious child, who loved to talk to anyone who would listen. His mum told *People* magazine how, when he was only four years old, he said to her: 'Mom, I'm gonna be on T.V., and I don't mean when I grow up.' His parents didn't know the first thing about how to get their son involved with acting, and so they tried their best to distract him with other activities, like sports and school. Little Johnny wasn't to be deterred, however. Eventually his parents started taking him to open-call auditions in Chicago. The move paid off, and at his first open-call Johnny 'hopped right up on the stage and sang something and got a role. From that point on they didn't try to put me in soccer or T-ball or anything.' By age seven he was on stage in productions of *Fiddler on the Roof* and *The Member of the Wedding*.

He got his television acting break in *Murder Ordained* (1987), a mini-series starring John Goodman, when he was twelve years old. He continued to read for roles from his home in Illinois, including for *National Lampoon's Christmas Vacation* in 1989, his first venture into comedy. 'I was 13, and I read for that role on tape.

They flew me out to read with Chevy Chase. They must have been really hard up; I'm not sure why I got that role…I wasn't bringing much comedic to the table whatsoever at 13,' Johnny told *The AV Club*. Still, he must have impressed the right people as he got the job! When it was clear that Johnny was set to make it big in Hollywood, his entire family moved out to Los Angeles. They stayed in a complex of purpose-built, fully-furnished apartments in Beverly Hills, where Johnny met other young actors and actresses like Jennifer Love Hewitt. After nine months in LA, Johnny's family decided that the California scene wasn't for them, and they moved back to Chicago. Johnny, on the other hand, decided to stay to finish up his contract on a show called *American Dreamer*, but by the time that was over he already had more work lined up and so he decided to stay, on his own, in Los Angeles. It was a scary time for young Johnny, 'It was actually quite intimidating and lonely, to be honest.'

Yet by staying out in Los Angeles, Johnny was developing the kind of connections that would carry him throughout his career. After being cast in the TV movie *Backfield in Motion* (1991), starring Roseanne Barr and Tom Arnold, Roseanne was so impressed by the young actor that she asked him to appear in her television show (also called *Roseanne*). It was only meant to be a small role: 'She got me an episode, to do one scene on the show. There wasn't much there to do. Kind of rile things up with Sara Gilbert. It wasn't a whole lot to study or create or crawl into,' he said to *The A.V. Club*. But the chemistry between Sara and Johnny was perfect, and his role broadened into a love interest, as Sara's character's boyfriend and then husband, David Healy: 'After that one episode, she asked me to do three more episodes, and then she asked me to do three years,' said Johnny.

It was a huge moment for Johnny, who had grown up watching the show religiously with the rest of his family. 'I remember watching the first episode [of *Roseanne*] sitting on the living room floor in my family's house in Chicago and my parents looking at one another afterwards and saying it was almost creepy. They felt like the writer's had been looking in our windows,' he told *The Culture Shock*. As a result he was hugely intimidated by the set and the actors. 'I was...surrounded by television heroes of mine,' he continued to *The A.V. Club*. Yet ironically, that nervous energy and fear which underlined his performance as David Healy actually worked for the character, and was a key factor in the extension of his role: 'That scared little rabbit that I was, observing all of this from the shadowy corners of the stage, was something the writers were brilliant enough to observe and inoculate into the character. Eventually, that became something. The way they wrote it and the way I played it. And it fortunately played so well off the Darlene character, too. My spinelessness and her strength.'

Roseanne was a part of Johnny's life for five years. In between breaks in the show's filming, he picked up bit parts in a few movies, including *Suicide Kings* and *I Know What You Did Last Summer*. He credits Jennifer Love Hewitt (the star of *I Know What You Did…*) for bringing him on board the film, as she knew him from his days living alone on the apartment complex. He also starred in *The Opposite of Sex* and *Bounce*, both by director Don Roos.

Once *Roseanne* was over, Johnny looked to go back to his roots and take part in another play. He was cast in *The Little Dog Laughed*, a Broadway play, which ran from 13 November 2006 to 18 February 2007. His character was a male prostitute, and he had to do a full-frontal nude scene! Still, Johnny had the time of his life, and Johnny came home with a 2007 Theatre World Award after the play closed.

While he was doing the play, Johnny once again

discovered the power of 'who you know' in an industry like acting. Johnny had crossed paths with a certain producer by the name of Chuck Lorre, who had just finished working on *Roseanne* as Johnny was starting out. Performing on Broadway in front of a live audience had re-awoken in Johnny the desire to do more audience-based work, and on television the only way to do that is with a sitcom. Television was also much more lucrative than a play would ever be, even if he won awards for doing it. It was as his play was wrapping up that he got a call from Chuck, who he had kept in contact with over the years. 'Chuck kind of called at the perfect time and told me about this idea that he had. He didn't have a script yet but he said let's keep talking about it and I'll send you a couple themes when we're done with them and we kept talking that way,' Johnny said to *The Culture Shock*.

Johnny was intrigued by the script when he first read it, and although Chuck wanted him to audition for Sheldon, Johnny thought that the character of Leonard Hofstadter would actually be the better fit. He was actually worried to tell Chuck his views: 'I kind of figured that he would tell me to screw off, but he was like "Ok, great." That was it.'

Johnny then flew back to L.A. to meet Chuck's co-creator Bill Prady and to start testing with other potential cast members. It was key for Chuck and Bill to get the chemistry right between their two leads. Once they found Jim Parsons to play Sheldon, they shot the original version of the pilot, which was rejected by the network. Still, Johnny had faith that this idea could be refined, and he stuck with Chuck and Bill as they re-wrote. 'It was a two, two-and-a-half year process to get it through from the time that Chuck called me till it finally aired. It was interesting,' Johnny laughed.

In the summer breaks between filming, Johnny had the time to fit in a couple of movies – including *Hancock* in 2008, with Will Smith, and *In Time* alongside Justin Timberlake and Amanda Seyfried in autumn 2011. But for now, *The Big Bang Theory* dominates Johnny's life.

Games

Sheldon, Leonard and the gang have several geek-tastic games that they play throughout the series. These include, among many others: 3D Chess, Klingon Boggle, Rock Paper Scissors Lizard Spock, Super Agent Laser Obstacle Chess and Trestling.

3D Chess

This is regular chess but played on a three-dimensional board, thereby requiring a bit more lateral thinking! 3D chess is not new to *The Big Bang Theory*, in fact, the earliest incarnation of 3D chess was invented in 1907 called 'Raumschach' (German for 'Space Chess'). The 3D chess set that is played by Sheldon and Leonard in *The Big Bang Theory* is the *Star Trek* Tri-Dimensional Chess variant – a popular past time for the Vulcans. Since Sheldon is an aspiring Vulcan, it is the perfect game for him!

Klingon Boggle

Boggle™ is a game with 4x4 grid of dice, each with a different letter on each side. The grid is shaken to randomise the letters, and players must make as many words as they can think of using a sequence of adjoining letters in a predetermined amount of time. In Klingon Boggle, the letters are all in Klingonese (a language invented by James Doohan for *Star Trek: The Motion Picture* and later expanded by Marc Okrand for *Star Trek III: The Search for Spock*) and words are judged by using a Klingon-English dictionary.

Rock Paper Scissors Lizard Spock

A variation on the traditional rock–paper–scissors game to include two additional variables. Apart from the normal rules, Spock can defeat Rock and Scissors, but is defeated by Paper and Lizard, while Lizard can rule over Spock and Paper but is defeated by Rock and Scissors. The problem is that none of the guys want to be anything other than Spock, and so games often end up in a stalemate. Jim Parsons, who plays Sheldon, finds this the most difficult game to play: '[My dialogue] is easy for the most part. Except for "Rock, paper, scissors, lizard, Spock." That was never easy.'

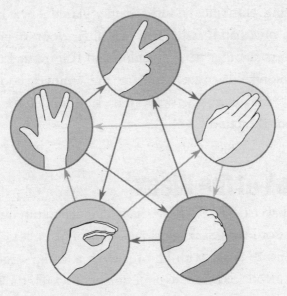

Secret Agent Laser Obstacle Chess

As if 3D chess wasn't enough, the *Big Bang* boys invent an additional challenge to the game of chess (which can reasonably be applied to any other board game, too!). A player must pass through a series of strategically positioned green laser beams without breaking any of them, in order to reach the board and make their next move. Best accompanied with an *a capella* rendition of 'The Sabre Dance' by composer Aram Khachaturian.

Trestling

A challenging test of strength and mental ability, trestling combines a Tetris battle, played on a laptop with one hand, with arm wrestling your opponent using your other hand. Sheldon and Raj trestled in the Cheesecake Factory, much to the annoyance of the other restaurant-goers (Season 1, Episode 16, 'The Peanut Reaction').

Geek of the Week

Every week, *The Big Bang Theory*'s resident astrophysicist, Professor David Saltzberg, invites one of his colleagues or students to come with him to watch a taping session of the show. 'I know a few professors who watch the show

– more than I would have expected – and they like it,' he explained to *UCLA Today*. This special person is allowed to come and stand down by the set along with the rest of the writers. Since Prof Saltzberg almost always invites a fellow physicist along, his special guest has become affectionately known amongst the crew as the 'geek of the week'.

Geeks (and Nerds and Dweebs)

The liberal use of the words 'geek' and 'nerd' in association with *The Big Bang Theory* has always been a controversial point. 'I was always kind of struggling with labeling the characters in a demeaning way because they're brilliant characters. But I guess "brilliant" isn't as good a word for the media as "geek" and "nerd",' Chuck said to *Collider* magazine. Bill Prady continued: 'there are two ways those words are used; one as a self-identification and of pride and then there's a derogatory aspect of it and we never approach the characters with labels. We said let's do a show about these people.' 'They're dimensionalised people,' chimed in Chuck, again. 'You can't simply say they're a "geek" or a "nerd" and be done with it.'

While Chuck and Bill deny that they are writing about

just 'geeks', it is certainly true that the show was launched on the crest of the wave of geek love that seemed to take over television in the late 2000's. CBS president Nina Tassler agreed in 2007: 'I think *The Big Bang Theory* reflects a shift in the cultural landscape…Groups of friends like this, with their type of "geek chic", have blossomed into a very familiar and relatable demographic. We're seeing it in film, in literature, and I think it's a fresh way to access comedy.'

The trend seemed to start in movies, with geek-focused comedies like *The 40 Year Old Virgin*, *Napoleon Dynamite* and *Superbad* dominating the box office. Then on came the rush of television series with geek-protagonists, like *Chuck* with Zachary Levi in the title role, about a slacker computer genius who accidentally has government secrets embedded into his brain, *Aliens in America*, featuring the gawky teenager Justin Tolchuck, played by Dan Byrd, and *Reaper*, whose main character, Sam (Bret Harrison), is a video-game-obsessed loser whose soul is sold to the devil by his parents.

So why such an influx of geek-related comedies? For the creator of *Chuck*, Josh Schwartz (who is also responsible for *The O.C.*), he refers back to the old adage of 'write what you know', 'and certainly, as [co-executive producer] Chris [Fedak] and I can attest, we know many more writers who resemble Chuck than, say, Jack Bauer [of *24*].' Of all the series mentioned (apart from *The Big Bang Theory*), *Chuck* is the only series still running, which just goes to show that it's not just about capturing the zeitgeist – there has to be something more to a show than just following a trend. There are even geek celebrities now, like both Apple co-founders Steve Jobs and Steve Wozniak, the latter of whom went on to appear in *Dancing with the Stars*.

It's been difficult for *Big Bang* creators Chuck Lorre and Bill Prady to accept that they are simply a part of a 'geek' trend, as they don't believe in defining their characters that way: 'I've always been against the whole idea of just calling them 'nerds,' because it doesn't define who they are…They are human beings. They have parents, and they have brothers and sisters and goals and fears – and they are geniuses,' said Chuck to *Deseret News*. 'It doesn't really give you any insight into them by giving them a name of 'nerd' or 'geek.' It doesn't begin to describe what they are. In fact, they are probably the characters who will change the world. They may blow it up, [but] that will be the change.'

The characters in *The Big Bang Theory* are definitely not 'geeks' in the same way as Justin, Bret and Chuck (the character, not the creator!) are because they are not in any way slackers. They have real jobs, and are actively involved in furthering their respective fields. The fact that they also happen to subscribe to geek culture is an indication of their passions outside of their work, not the main driving force of their life.

It's a fine distinction to make, but an important one. It's also a line that the writer's have to walk very close to with each script. They are constantly learning when the script goes overboard with geek-references. 'It really is a guessing game as to what's too much and also just being true to the characters,' said Chuck Lorre in a *Television Without Pity* interview. 'You know, you just look at every line of dialogue in every story and say, "Is this legitimate for our show?" And also if it can be done by another show then it's not our show. If it's just a story about a group of guys hanging out, well they're not just a group of guys. They're extraordinary guys. And if we're not reflecting that then it's not.'

The balancing act is not only for the characters' benefit, but for the benefit of the audience too. 'If the show becomes too reference heavy then I think it risks losing a lot of people who are not deeply immersed in the minutia of nerddom…every decision is a guess, really. Where is the line? What's too much? What's enough? What's just right?'

It's been a learning process, and one that the whole cast and crew have been coming to terms with. For Johnny Galecki, who plays Leonard, it's been something of a revelation: 'One of the things I've learned from this show is that people who are sometimes called "nerds" or "geeks" or "dweebs" are really just people who are passionate about something. And ultimately, passion is appealing, even if the subject is something you're personally not passionate about' (CBS *Watch!* magazine).

Despite the geek-love in and around Hollywood, the cast do get a bit of ribbing from the general public – but they take it all in their stride. For Johnny Galecki, it's nothing compared to the taunts he received while starring on *Roseanne*, when people on the street would constantly shout at him 'Where's Darlene?' (in reference to his on-screen girlfriend). In fact, the only incident Galecki can remember was at a basketball game: 'There was just one time, when we had really good seats at a Lakers game, and some jock was jealous. He yelled, "NERDS!",' he said to *Watch!* magazine. Kaley Cuoco then added: 'And you were like, "Whatever! We're the nerds on the FLOOR!"' And Johnny was right: nerds have taken over the world; it's definitely hip to be square.

Gilbert, Sara

Sara Gilbert plays the hilarious nemesis to Sheldon and sometime lover of Leonard and Howard, Dr. Leslie Winkle, an optical physicist. Sara Gilbert has a longstanding relationship with creator of the show, Chuck Lorre, which goes back right to her days as a star in the sitcom *Roseanne*.

Sara Gilbert was born Sara Rebecca Abeles on 29 January 1975. She had two adoptive siblings from her mother's first marriage, Melissa and Jonathan Gilbert, who were also in the acting business. Sara changed her last name to Gilbert once she made the decision to act.

Her big break came at only thirteen, in 1988, when she was cast as Darlene Conner in *Roseanne*. She stayed with the show until it ended its run in 1997, even managing to complete a college degree at Yale in art (with an emphasis on photography), while remaining on the show full-time.

But Sara isn't the only connection between *Roseanne* and *The Big Bang Theory*. Chuck Lorre worked on the show from 1990–1992 as a writer and producer. Also, Johnny Galecki (Leonard), played Sara's boyfriend, and eventually husband on the show, David Healy. It was therefore a real thrill for Johnny when Chuck decided to hire her. 'It's always a luxury to work with someone

Sara Gilbert, who plays Dr. Leslie Winkle

you already share a creative shorthand with. Initially Chuck, Sara and I wondered if having her on the show might appear gimmicky. But she was just the best actress for the role. Plus, selfishly, who wouldn't want to work with someone they personally and professionally adore? On the downside, Gilbert is the only person in a position to gauge any lack of progress I've made as a kisser over the last 16 years.'

Although by the second season it looked as if Sara would becoming a regular cast member on *The Big Bang Theory*, her role was dropped back down to 'recurring'. When some fans became a bit confused as the future of Leslie Winkle, television journalist Michael Ausiello decided to dig a bit deeper. He spoke to an insider on the show, and in one of his weekly 'Ausiello Reports' he shared that the writers were finding it hard to write storylines for the character, and had decided to cut back her airtime rather than force a plot that wouldn't necessarily fit with the rest of the show.

Glau, Summer

Summer Glau is a beautiful American television actress best known for playing River Tam in sci-fi series *Firefly*

SUMMER GLAU, WHO
GUEST-STARRED ON *THE
BIG BANG THEORY*

and accompanying feature film *Serenity*, and the cyborg Cameron in *Terminator: The Sarah Connor Chronicles*. When Chuck Lorre and Bill Prady were dreaming up storylines, they wondered what it would be like if the guys met a goddess of the science fiction universe. 'Narrowing it down to those who were available and who were willing to have a sense of humour about themselves led us to Summer – fortunate, because she was also our first choice!' laughed Bill Prady to *Variety*.

Bill actually approached his friend (and the creator of *Terminator: The Sarah Connor Chronicles*), Josh Friedman, before they approached Summer, to gauge how she might react to the invite. 'When I talked to him [Bill], he said, '"Do you think Summer would want to play Summer?" The script was really funny and the idea was really funny. I was at the read-through and I wanted to go when they were actually shooting, but I thought it would be a little weird. I didn't want to be like the protective parent, the stage dad or something,' said Josh. He told Bill to go for it, and so he offered Summer the role, which she gladly accepted.

Summer was thrilled to be asked to guest star, but found it a challenge to do comedy when she had only previously done dramatic work. 'I think that I was playing myself, but I was trying to be funny, they tried to make me funny,' she recalled to *Comic Book Resources*. 'I was nervous, because it's supposed to be about how I respond to people who know my work as Cameron, so I was concerned about how people might perceive that. But I was honored to work with such talented actors.'

Summer Glau isn't the only famous sexy sci-fi guest star that *The Big Bang Theory* has featured. Viewers have also been treated to Katee Sackhoff, who is best known in the sci-fi world as Captain Kara 'Starbuck' Thrace in *Battlestar Galactica*. She has appeared so far in two episodes as Howard Wolowitz's conscience/dream girl. Another guest star is Eliza Dushku, of *Buffy the Vampire Slayer* and *Dollhouse* fame. She came on to *The Big Bang Theory* set as an FBI agent who is checking out all of Howard Wolowitz's friends before he can gain top security clearance for his job. What is it with *The Big Bang Theory* producers surrounding Wolowitz with all the beautiful women? Maybe he is more of a ladies man than we think! As for Eliza, she made sure to come fully prepared for her role: 'I am a fan [of the show], but I have to be honest. I Wikipedia-ed each of their characters to see things that have been revealed and things that might be in their file so I would get lines that I wouldn't have made the connection to because I haven't watched every single episode,' said Eliza to TVGuide.com.

KATEE SACKHOFF, WHO HAS GUEST-STARRED IN THREE *BIG BANG THEORY* EPISODES

There are many other famous women of science fiction who would make great stars – maybe Liv Tyler, who played Arwen in *Lord of the Rings*, or Lena Heady, who has immense geek-cred from her starring roles as Sarah Connor in *Terminator: The Sarah Connor Chronicles* and as Cersei Lannister in HBO's *Game of Thrones*. What with *The Big Bang Theory*'s profile rising, there's no limit to the great guest stars they could get to come on board!

Helberg, Simon

Simon Maxwell Helberg never thought of himself as a nerd – not until he got cast as Howard Wolowitz, that is. He first wondered if he wasn't quite as cool as he thought was when he went in for his audition: 'It's funny because I used to sort of like have shaggy, Beatlesy hair. And that was cool, I thought. And then I went into the audition, and they were like, "Oh, my God, and your hair, it was perfect. It was so nerdy. Like, keep it like that",' he laughed to CTV.

Simon couldn't have a much cooler background,

SIMON HELBERG
(HOWARD WOLOWITZ)
WITH HIS WIFE,
JOCELYN TOWNE

however. His dad is the German-American actor Sandy Helberg, who teamed up with Mel Brooks in three films (*High Anxiety*, *History of the World: Part 1* and *Spaceballs*) and who established the L.A. improv troupe The Groundlings, and his mother, Harriet, is a respected casting director and writer. With parents so heavily involved in the acting world, it seemed like he was destined to be an actor since birth. But in actuality, Simon took quite a bit of time to come to that decision – he wasn't one of those children that knew from age three he wanted to be an actor.

Simon was born on 9 December 1980 in Los Angeles. As a kid, he was actually more into playing music then he was acting. He is an accomplished piano player and he joined or started a lot of rock bands throughout his early years of high school. He also thought himself something of a future Karate Kid. 'When I was ten I was a black belt in Karate, actually,' he told *Fancast*. 'I saw *The Karate Kid* and I was like this is what I have to do and from the time I was five-and-a-half I just started going to karate like at all hours of the day and by the time I was ten I was a black belt.' But by the time he hit the eleventh grade, around age 15–16, he started auditioning for some of his high school plays. His natural inclination was to turn straight to comedy – he had been immersed in that world since birth, growing up with his father and hanging around watching The Groundlings do improv. But his drama teacher challenged him to break outside his box: 'The first time I did a scene, my main acting teacher there said, "You're not allowed to do any comedy for the rest of the year because you clearly feel comfortable doing that and I don't want you to feel comfortable. Making you uncomfortable is what acting is about."' Pushing him out of his comfort zone turned out to be the right thing to do for Simon. He fell in love with the craft, and wanted to learn more. For that, he turned to the Tisch School of Arts program in New York City, in association with the Atlantic Theatre School. The three-year Bachelor of Fine Arts program has seen many of its alumni go on to make it on screens both small and big, like Felicity Huffman (*Desperate Housewives*), and Jessica Alba (*Dark Angel*, *Fantastic Four*).

From 1999, Simon was working continuously on TV in guest roles in shows as varied as *Popular* and *Sabrina, the Teenage Witch*. But in 2002 he got the opportunity to work with some of his on-screen comedy idols on *MadTV*, which he joined as a feature performer. Just as his high school drama teacher had seen, comedy just felt right for Simon. Unfortunately, *MadTV* didn't end up being the right show for him: 'I kind of grew up with [improv] in my bones, with my dad and all. I was doing a lot of it in Los Angeles at "Second City" out here, and I spent a few years performing and I really fell in love with it. As for *MadTV*, it was a bit disheartening – it really wasn't my cup of tea the way they ran everything over there. I enjoyed the experience, I was 22 and it was a real kind of bureaucratic system, and it just…there was a lot of talent there, but it was really challenging to get your vision of something on the air…the sketch[es] seemed insurmountable and really infinite.' Still, Simon didn't let the experience put him off too much, and he continued getting bit parts in television shows until his next break.

That came in 2006 with *Studio 60 on the Sunset Strip*, ironically a comedy about what goes on behind the scenes of an improvised comedy show like *MadTV* or *Saturday Night Live*. Simon played Alex Dwyer, one of the fictional show's ensemble cast, known for his impression of Nicholas Cage. It was interesting for Simon, having come from that world, to doing a comedy about it, and he was well-placed to see whether *Studio 60* was doing a good depiction: 'I thought there were a lot of aspects about the sketch comedy world that were relevant and accurate in a way [in *Studio 60*]…I had a great time doing it…It was a little hectic, it was a little chaotic, but I was loving being around everybody and doing that work. So, yeah, overall, it was very fantastic – and it led right into *The Big Bang Theory*!'

Since being cast as the wannabe Casanova Howard Wolowitz, Simon's life has changed forever. 'The best part has been meeting all these wonderful people I get to work with. They have become some of my best friends.' A less attractive side-effect has been his unfortunate hair-style, which is his real hair and not a wig. Luckily, Simon takes it all in stride and knows it's a small sacrifice to make for a successful show: 'They flat-iron [my hair], and it looks more like Moe Howard as opposed to John Lennon, hopefully. So I've embraced it. I enjoy looking kind of as bad as I possibly can,' laughs Simon.

Hofstadter, Leonard Leakey

Dr. Leonard Leakey Hofstadter, PhD, is an experimental physicist employed at Caltech. He is often depicted at work using lasers, and his roommate Sheldon frequently

DR. LEONARD HOFSTADTER IS PLAYED BY JOHNNY GALECKI

lambasts him for not coming up with original research and essentially copying that of others. Of course, Sheldon doesn't really mean that Leonard actually plagiarises other people's work, but he is still demeaning Leonard's research (and intelligence) anyway!

Ironically, despite him appearing like a genius to most people, Leonard is actually considered the underachiever in his family. His mother, Dr. Beverly Hofstadter, is a neuroscientist and psychiatrist who constantly analyses everyone she interacts with. She gets along well with Sheldon as a result. His sister is a medical researcher, while his brother, Michael, is a Harvard law professor. Leonard was born and raised in New Jersey.

Leonard is probably the least socially awkward of his group of friends, and immediately falls for Penny when she moves in across the hall, which is the catalyst for the entire show. 'I think [Leonard], to me, is the emotional center of the show,' said Bill Prady to *Variety*. 'Penny tugs Leonard out into the world, and Sheldon tugs him away from the world. Leonard and Sheldon are near the middle, not the extremes, and Koothrappali and Wolowitz bracket them on either side.' Leonard is not as crazy as Sheldon, and his relative normality makes him more relatable. He just wants to fit in.

Leonard's first name is derived from famed television producer Sheldon Leonard, and his last name from the late Robert Hofstadter, who won the Nobel Prize in Physics in 1961. He is played by Johnny Galecki.

Hop

Hop is a part-animated feature comedy film that was released on 1 April 2011 and starred Kaley Cuoco and James Marsden in live-action roles and Russell Brand and Hugh Hefner as voices. Kaley plays Sam, the ambitious younger sister to James Marsden's slacker Fred. Fred goes on to meet the son of the Easter Bunny (E.B.), which changes all of their lives forever. The E.B. was completely CGI, which meant Kaley had the unique experience of acting opposite a beanbag: 'It was a black bag with sand and fake little arms,' she told *Collider* magazine. 'We did a take of that, and then we did a take with a stuffed animal that looked exactly like E.B. It was very strange.'

It was Kaley's first big role in a movie since she started on *The Big Bang Theory*. 'I'm so excited,' said Kaley. 'Last summer, I was ready to do a film, and this one came along. It was just the most fun experience. I've really got the film bug now, and I hope that takes me somewhere in my life as well. I'd never say this for sure, but I think I've built a name in television, and my next step is to find a place in the film world. There are all these goals I have, and I've met my television goal, so I want to reach some others.'

She really enjoyed working with James Marsden too, although she found shooting a film after doing a sitcom for so long a complete change of pace. To occupy themselves during downtime, she and James would play lots of games: 'Doing a film, we would do one scene, all day. I was like, "These guys are slow. This is crazy!" We would get really giddy, by the end of the day, because they were really long, and I was just bad, off camera. I was constantly making faces. We played a lot of Words with Friends on our iPhones. We played Scrabble, constantly.'

The movie opened to poor critical reviews but huge box office numbers. Since it's always the money that talks, Kaley can expect to have options for acting on the big screen for years to come!

I

I am I

In between shooting the upcoming seasons of *The Big Bang Theory*, Simon Helberg is working on a project called *I am I* with his wife, writer, actress and filmmaker Jocelyn Towne. *I am I* is an interesting project because it is being funded through an experimental platform known as KickStarter. KickStarter was designed as a launch pad for people to test products. Innovators behind creative projects of all kinds – from jewellery design to inventions to bands to movies – put up pitches on the website, and website goers are able to choose which projects they are inspired by and want to see happen. Those people then, hopefully, put their money where their mouths are and vote with their wallet. Simon and Jocelyn's aim was to raise $100,000 toward the film. They dropped in small incentives into the programme, so that people who donated from $100 were credited at the end of the movie, and so on. 'It is a way to make people and the fans act as the studio for the movie. These are the people that are going to see the movie, so why not have them help us make it and actually invest in it. You become a team early on. It has been a great experience,' said Simon to *Media Gate*.

The premise of *I am I* is about a young woman named Rachel who meets her long-lost father at her mother's funeral. But because her father suffers from retrograde amnesia, he believes that the Rachel is in fact her mother. Rachel allows her father to believe the delusion so that she can figure out why he abandoned her and her mother. Reading the script was a strange experience for Simon. He told MSN Canada: 'It was weird because I thought, "Oh gosh, what if I read this and it's not good, and how do I deal with my wife? But in all honesty it blew me away.' Simon and Jocelyn announced on 1 February 2011 that the fundraising venture for *I am I* had been successful and that they had reached their goal, meaning we will hopefully be seeing *I am I* in theatres soon!

Inter-cast Dating

Whenever a couple has a lot of chemistry on set, it's bound to spill over into speculation about their real lives. There was no exception for Johnny Galecki and Kaley Cuoco, whose characters Leonard and Penny sparkled with chemistry. But from the cast members themselves there was nothing but denial, denial, denial.

In 2010, however, Kaley Cuoco announced that she and Johnny had been dating for two years – the key point being the past tense 'had' – they had broken up just before Christmas 2009 in the middle of the show's third season (ironically just when their characters had started dating properly). They had managed to keep their relationship under wraps and out of the public eye all that time – a truly remarkable feat for what would be such a high profile story. 'It was a wonderful relationship but we never spoke a word about it and never went anywhere together,' said Kaley to CBS *Watch!* magazine. 'We were so protective of ourselves and the show and didn't want anything to ruin that. But that also made it sad, too.

That's not the kind of relationship I want – I don't want to be hiding.'

It's very lucky that the two have managed to stay friends, and they are such professionals that they haven't let any residual emotion mar their on-screen chemistry. After the relationship, though, Kaley swore off dating her fellow kind: 'No more actors … I've dated so many actors… I've got to be done with that.' Kaley is now dating Christopher French from the indie rock band Annie Automatic, while Johnny Galecki is still keeping mum on his relationship status.

The IT Crowd

The IT Crowd is a hit British sitcom which offers some similarities to *The Big Bang Theory*. Created by Graham Linehan of such great British sitcoms as *Father Ted* and *Black Books*, it features the nerdy genius Maurice Moss (played with aplomb by Richard Ayoade), his techie workmate Roy Tenneman (Chris O'Dowd) and their boss Jen Barber (Katherine Parkinson), who is completely computer illiterate but becomes friends with her two geeky co-workers despite not knowing anything about IT herself.

The show films in front of a live audience, and was

RICHARD AYOADE, WHO PLAYS MOSS IN *THE IT CROWD*

Linehan's answer to rumours that the sitcom-format was dead. *IT Crowd* ran for four seasons with six episodes per season, with a fifth season in production. It premiered on 3 February 2006, to initially low ratings, but it has built in popularity ever since.

Like *The Big Bang Theory*, *The IT Crowd* set is littered with geek culture references, and the two main characters love video games, MMORPGs (Massively Multiplayer Online Role Playing Games like *World of Warcraft*) and comics. Yet without the massive budget that *The Big Bang Theory* has, and unable to source the props he wanted under tight time constraints, Graham wrote on his blog asking for the fans of the show to send in their own geeky memorabilia: 'I'm talking about posters, comics, fanzines, T-shirts…anything you've seen in the last few months that you think is pretty cool or captures the spirit of the show or a particular character…[N]ormally I'd delight in tracking down the stuff myself, but as I say, it's just not going to happen this time round…I wanted it to feel like a geek Shangri-La, and in each series I've felt we nearly got there. Maybe this time, with you guys involved, we'll finally nail it.' The call was answered, and Graham received tons of extra props, including loads of 1970s and '80s computer manuals from The Centre of Computing History.

A US version of *The IT Crowd* was brought to networks around the same time as *The Big Bang Theory*. Ayoade was brought in to reprise his role as Moss and the script for the pilot was mostly the same as the British version, although Linehan himself had very little to do with the production. Yet although NBC were initially enthusiastic about the prospect and ordered an entire season, the show was cancelled before any episodes aired on TV. Despite not having much to do with the development, Linehan was disappointed when it failed to take off. In an interview with *Den of Geek*, Linehan compared his show to *The Big Bang Theory*: 'the way I wanted to see *The IT Crowd* work in America is actually *The Big Bang Theory*, you know?…[*The Big Bang Theory*] is not perfect at the moment but I think it'll get better and better. It's going to be one of the big shows – might be the next *Friends* or something… I felt a huge admiration for the show, but also really annoyed that people didn't see that that's what *The* [US] *IT Crowd* could have been. It just frustrated me a little bit.'

Japanese Anime

In Season 3, Episode 3, 'The Gothowitz Deviation', Sheldon and Leonard introduce Penny to the world of Japanese anime. In a bit of a Chuck Lorre inside joke, Sheldon says they are watching *Oshikuru: Demon Samurai*, which is the same show that Charlie Sheen's character writes a jingle theme for in *Two and a Half Men*. In reality, the anime they are watching is *Boogiepop Phantom*, a hit anime television series from 2000.

Joyner, Eric and other artists

Art is featured all over the walls of *The Big Bang Theory* set, frequently from well-known sci-fi artists. One such artist is Eric Joyner, a San Francisco-based artist known for his whimsical renditions of robots battling donuts. Several pieces of his art hang around Sheldon and Leonard's apartment, including a piece called 'Caught Again' which hangs above Leonard's bed and 'Rockem Sockem' which is hung on the door to their closet in the living room.

Other artists featured include Michael Saul (and his painting 'Robots Exploring the Desert'), Frank R. Paul (who designed a *War of the Worlds*-inspired magazine cover for *Amazing Stories* in 1927, which hangs in the apartment hallway) and Brandon Ragnar Johnson, a Vegas-based artist whose comic-book style posters for the comic book store House of Night feature prominently in Sheldon's bedroom.

K

Koothrappali, Priya

Priya Koothrappali is Raj's sister. She lives in India like her parents, and works as a Cambridge-educated corporate lawyer. When she was introduced to the gang, Leonard and Howard are immediately attracted to her, and swear to each other than neither will make a move. That being said, Leonard and Priya end up sleeping together, and continue to do so whenever Priya is in town visiting Raj from India. However, Leonard starts developing deeper feelings for Priya and even suggests that he move over to India at one point.

Instead, they start a relationship when she moves over to the U.S., much to the annoyance of Raj. Priya is played by Aarti Mann.

Koothrappali, Rajesh Ramayan

Dr. Rajesh 'Raj' Ramayan Koothrappali, PhD., is a particle astrophysicist working at Caltech. He was named one of *People* magazine's 'Top 30 Under 30' for his discovery of a planetary object beyond the Kuiper belt. His best friend is Howard Wolowitz, and he lives on his own in a small apartment in Pasadena.

Raj was born and raised in New Delhi, India. He has a big family and is still close with his parents, Dr. V.M. and Mrs. Koothrappali, with whom he communicates regularly on his laptop via webcam.

One of Raj's defining traits is his selective mutism – he is unable to talk to women unless he is under the influence of alcohol. The only woman he can speak to easily is his mother. Ironically, when he does speak to women he is probably the most successful of the group when it comes to getting ladies. He can be very suave and persuasive when he believes he is drunk – he just has to learn how to translate that charm into sober situations!

Above: The main *Big Bang Theory* cast – Jim Parsons (Sheldon), Simon Helberg (Howard), Kaley Cuoco (Penny), Kunal Nayyar (Rajesh) and Johnny Galecki (Leonard).

Below: Simon Helberg, Melissa Rauch (who plays Howard's love interest, Bernadette), Kunal Nayyar and Mayim Bialik (who plays Amy Farrah Fowler).

Our favourite *Big Bang* friends!

Above left: Johnny Galecki (looking much cooler than his character, Leonard!)

Above right: Simon Helberg

Below left: Kunal Nayyar

Below right: Jim Parsons

Kaley Cuoco (Penny)
looking gorgeous on
the red carpet at the
Golden Globe Awards.

Above: *Big Bang Theory* co-creator Chuck Lorre with the cast of one of his most famous creations, *Two and a Half Men*.

Below left: Former *Blossom* star Mayim Bialik was mentioned on *The Big Bang Theory* before she'd even auditioned to join the cast.

Below right: Sara Gilbert, who plays Dr. Leslie Winkle, also worked with Chuck Lorre and Johnny Galecki on *Roseanne*.

Above: Jim Parsons, who plays the eccentric Dr. Sheldon Cooper, is a fans' favourite and has won countless awards for his role in *The Big Bang Theory*.

Below: The cast are in hot demand and are always attending celebrity parties and awards ceremonies.

Above: Barenaked Ladies, the band who performed *The Big Bang Theory*'s theme song, 'The History of Everything'.

Below: *The Big Bang Theory* has had a string of famous guest stars, such as Katee Sackhoff (*left*) and Summer Glau (*right*).

ANIZAL
APL

Surprisin

Big Bang star Simon
Helberg with his wife,
actress Jocelyn Towne.

Above left: Eliza Dushku, another sexy sci-fi star who has made a guest appearance on *The Big Bang Theory*!

Above right: Kunal Nayyar out and about meeting fans in LA.

Below: In real life Kaley Cuoco always looks glamorous – unlike her character, Penny, who can usually be found wearing tracksuits or her Cheesecake Factory uniform!

Kunal Nayyar, who plays Dr. Rajesh Koothrappali

Raj is played by Kunal Nayyar, who describes Raj as 'a geek–nerd who is a nerd–geek. He is just a very smart guy who lives in a bubble and doesn't really care what is going on around him as long as particle physics is evolving his life is good.'

Kripke, Barry

Barry Kripke is a rival physicist of Sheldon and Leonard at Caltech university, who is constantly antagonising them. He suffers from rhotacism, which makes it difficult for him to pronouce the letter 'r' (similar to Elmer Fudd in the *Looney Tunes* cartoons). He is best known for producing monster fighting robots, such as The Crippler.

He is played by John Ross Bowie.

JOHN ROSS BOWIE, WHO PLAYS BARRY KRIPKE

L

Learning Lines

Thanks to its scientifc nature, *The Big Bang Theory* has more complicated dialogue than most! It makes the actors' job especially challenging. This is especially true for Jim Parsons, whose character – Sheldon – has some of the longest and most complex monologues of all the characters. It's something that stood out to the network's president, Peter Roth, and part of what really impressed him about Jim: 'He has long monologues of these remarkable quantum theorems that you can barely pronounce let alone get out of your mouth,' he said to the *LA Times*. The difficulty is also compounded by the fact that he often doesn't have long to memorise the script, with filming taking place each week. Jim's trick? He writes the words out longhand – a technique he learned during his MA course: 'I write out all my lines again and again and again. And on the weekends, I drill them. I walk around with my note cards for each scene and do one scene at a time. And I'll go to my computer, and I'll type the whole scene out on my word doc and then I'll go back and I'll do the second scene, and I'll type the whole scene out on a word doc. It's maddening. I will not lie to you. I literally want to kill myself sometimes,' he laughed to MovieLine.com. He also takes to looking up any terms or physics theories he's not sure about on Wikipedia to get the condensed version!

But for Jim, it's all about finding the funny side of it all, as well as understanding the science – after all, it is a comedy program. Sheldon's particular (and peculiar) dialogue helps Jim to make the character appear so natural: 'The rhythm of the language they've written for Sheldon, I love that challenge,' Parsons said to the *LA Times*. 'The writers are so good at using so many words and scientific jargon and being verbose in general and burying the joke in there. The challenge of threading that out, driving these speeches in a way it still hits the comic rhythm, I love it, though I want to pull my hair out sometimes.' Jim even goes the added step of putting a pencil in his mouth in order to practice the very specific 'Sheldon' way of speaking.

Jim's little quirks have worked for other cast members too: writing out lines long-hand is a trick that Johnny Galecki has picked up. He even uses it when the writers make last-minute script adjustments, sometimes so last-minute that they occur in front of the live audience. It doesn't change Johnny's process, though: 'Even with the audience there, I say, "Give me 30 seconds" and write it out in longhand,' he told *Movie Line*.

The only cast member who doesn't need any tricks or prompts to learn lines is seasoned pro Kaley Cuoco. 'I don't know how she does it,' Jim said to the *LA Times*, 'but she always has every single word memorised.'

Leonard, Sheldon

Sheldon Leonard was a big time television producer and actor of the early twentieth century. He featured in movies like *To Have and Have Not* (1944) and *It's a Wonderful Life* (1946), but is best known for producing television shows like *The Dick Van Dyke Show* and *The Andy Griffith Show*. He passed away in 1997. Chuck Lorre and Bill Prady decided to name their two main characters after Sheldon Leonard as a tribute to the producer: 'There was just a little hero worship on our part there,' said Chuck Lorre to *Deseret News*. In Vanity Card #187, shown after the credits at the end of Chuck's TV shows, Chuck wrote from the point-of-view of the 'ghost of Sheldon Leonard', claiming that he was the one who was implanting the ideas for sitcoms in Chuck's brain – but Chuck was getting them all wrong!

Leakey, Louis

Louis Seymour Bazett Leakey (7 August 1903 – 1 October 1972) was a famous anthropologist who set about to prove Darwin's hypothesis that humans originated in Africa. He and his second wife Mary discovered the *Homo habilis* species in the Olduvai Gorge in Kenya.

Louis Leakey was the inspiration for Leonard 'Leakey' Hofstader's middle name.

Live Audience

Part of what makes *The Big Bang Theory* so great is that it is filmed in front of a live studio audience – there's no laughter track here. Every week, normally on a Tuesday night, a lucky group of TV enthusiasts get to watch the actors perform each episode live at the Warner Brothers Studios in Burbank, California, on Stage 25. Sheldon, Leonard and the rest would be proud – that stage also saw the filming of geek-friendly classics as the *Batman* movies and *Blade Runner*. Across the way is Studio 24, where *Friends* was filmed (and now nick-named the 'Friends stage'), and next door is *Two and a Half Men*. It's sitcom heaven!

Now that the show is well established with a huge fan base, the audience has become even more responsive to the characters and the jokes, and even learned to anticipate the punchlines. The characters had become like family to fans, who tuned in week after week and grew to learn their quirks and mannerisms almost as well as the actors themselves. It really struck home for Jim toward the end of the first season: 'The live audience started coming in and laughing before the joke was delivered. And it was really weird at first. Not completely unpleasant, but it was weird,' he said to *Buzzy Multimedia*. 'It was only completely pleasant when we all talked about it and realised what was happening – that they knew the characters and they knew what was coming. And I should have realised – oh, my God, it's the essence of television is, you want to tune in…It's not a movie, it's not a play, it's every week. And that was the first thing where I felt, "I feel I'm a part of something now that I didn't even know about before."'

As for Chuck Lorre and the writers, they are consistently amazed when the audience seems to get the nerdy references they put in: 'They respond to *Battlestar Galactica* references and old sci-fi references. They knew what *The Time Machine* was last year. And what a Morlock is,' he told *Television Without Pity*. 'So when we shoot the show on Tuesday nights…it's really fun cause the people in the audience are really excited to be there and their response is gratifying. I don't know if that's the same response to people that aren't necessarily living and breathing this kind of material.'

The audience is also necessary for the writers to establish whether they might have crossed the line with a particular scene or piece of dialogue. For Chuck, it's especially poignant when he has just come off the *Two and a Half Men* set and onto *The Big Bang Theory* – if he ever starts slipping into *Men*-style voice, the audience reacts audibly: 'Then…you know you've made a mistake,' said Chuck to *Collider*. 'We've re-written stuff in front of the audiences; we do that all the time anyway but it's very important to keep things separate.'

For Kaley, she relishes every day that they get to have a live taping. The energy that the audience brings 'makes the show's taping nights really fun…every crowd is like a rock concert'.

Lorre, Chuck

There's no disputing that Chuck Lorre is the king of modern day sitcoms. With not one, two but three of his mega-hit television shows currently on the air (*The Big Bang Theory*, *Two and a Half Men* and *Mike & Molly*), and even more in his back catalogue (like *Grace Under Fire*, *Cybill* and *Dharma & Greg*), he has managed to reinvigorate the genre when most others had written it off as a no-hoper. How Chuck manages to juggle it all is a mystery even to Lee Aronsohn, one of Lorre's co-creators on *Two and a Half Men* and *The Big Bang Theory*: 'Chuck is pretty hands on with all three shows…it's an ever-evolving system, and the best that can be said about it is that, so far, it seems to be working', Lee told the *Kansas City Star*. Even Lorre is

BIG BANG THEORY CREATOR CHUCK LORRE

not quite sure how he does it: 'You learn as you go…It's really gratifying and rewarding at times – but mostly, it's terrifying.'

Regardless, it's pretty good going for the young boy born Charles Michael Levine in Long Island, New York on 18 October 1952. His dad, Robert, owned a luncheonette (a diner-style cafe where patrons could sit on barstools while eating a quick lunch), but found it difficult to make enough money to keep his business open, even with Chuck jumping into the role of short-order cook at a tender 12-years-old. In a 2007 interview with *EW*, Chuck told of how his life changed after things got so bad that his mother had to take a retail job at a clothing store called Lorie's to help with their finances: 'My life changed dramatically… My dad struggled, and it hurt her very much. Anger was a big part of who she was.' It was not a happy childhood for Chuck, who said his was youth 'bereft of love' (*Los Angeles Times*). Instead, as soon as he could, Chuck turned to music. He continued to the *LA Times*: 'I also saw Jimi Hendrix light a guitar on fire when I was 17 and that kind of explosive power – what rock and roll can do – it made a big impact…Music was everything back then. TV was nothing. TV was *Bewitched* and *My Mother the Car*. When you had the Stones, the Beatles,

Dylan, Hendrix, Janis Joplin, Airplane, The Doors and The Who – television? Come on!'

Chuck tried college but dropped out after getting too caught up in the music scene and drugs to pursue any serious degree. But with music as the love of his life, he wrote songs for a living and travelled around the country with his guitar as a musician-for-hire.

Life got serious for Chuck when he had his two children, Asa and Nikki. He realised that he had to find a steady job, or else he would end up unable to feed his family: 'When they were born, I was determined to take care of them, no matter what,' he told *LA Independent*. With the goal of a long-term career in mind, Chuck turned his hand to television writing. He sent through lots of scripts, and got a job writing for animation shows for Marvel (where he met Stan Lee, who would come to guest star in *The Big Bang Theory*).

Incredibly, when you think about just how much Chuck Lorre has achieved in his television lifetime, his TV career didn't start until he was 35. But his big break wasn't until 1990, when he was taken aboard the writing team of *Roseanne*, set to become one of the biggest sitcoms of the Nineties. It was a turbulent few years for Chuck, whose relationship with titular actress Roseanne Barr was stormy at best. They were two strong characters, with their own ideas about how the story should evolve: 'She was ferociously determined to tell us how the story should be…One of the benefits of working 70 hours a week in hell is that the mind covers itself so you can't remember it,' said Lorre to *EW*.

Two years was enough for Lorre, and he moved on to *Grace Under Fire* (1993), starring actress Brett Butler and *Cybill* (with Cybill Shepherd) in 1995. *Cybill* in particular won great critical acclaim, garnering Emmys and Golden Globes for its stars Cybill Shepherd and Christine Baranski. Yet still, Lorre's working life was not easy and his behind-the-scenes clashes with the strong female leads in all his shows were well publicised.

All the drama led Chuck to create a show about warmth, friendliness and a happy-go-lucky woman: *Dharma & Greg*, starring Jenna Elfman and Thomas Gibson. It was during this show that Chuck aired his first 'vanity card', for which he was soon to become synonymous.

These massive successes led Warner Bros to sign Chuck up to a multi-million dollar deal. This was incredible news for Chuck, but meant that he took a step back from the day-to-day writing life of *Dharma & Greg*, which is seen as the beginning of the end for the show. But even bigger things were on the horizon, and

Chuck teamed up with his former *Roseanne* colleague Lee Aronsohn to write a new pilot: *Two and a Half Men*.

'It's no accident, and he'll even tell you this, that Chuck finally decided to do a show about men,' said the *Two and a Half Men* star Charlie Sheen to *EW* in 2007. *Two and a Half Men* is about a hedonistic, womanising man (Charlie Harper, played by Charlie Sheen), his newly divorced and uptight brother Alan (played by John Cryer) and Alan's son (Angus T. Jones), all living together in Charlie Harper's apartment. It debuted on 23 September 2003, and has been high in the comedy ratings ever since. His massive success with *Two and a Half Men* enabled Chuck to approach the network with even more ideas, which is how *The Big Bang Theory* and then more recently *Mike & Molly* were born. How on earth does one man sustain three ratings–busting shows? Apparently the secret is just to work really, really hard: 'It's just throwing yourself into it and giving everything you've got,' said Chuck to *Deseret News*. 'The opportunity to get a show on the air is so rare that you have to give it everything you've got because these chances, they don't come up very often, especially now. There's very few opportunities for comedies to get on the air anymore. So you throw yourself into it with sort of a neurotic abandon.'

But, it seems like Chuck had no better luck with

male divas than with his strong women as, at the moment, it seems like Chuck is even more famous now for his battles with Charlie Sheen than his shows. Charlie Sheen (born Carlos Irwin Estévez) had been best known for his role in sitcom *Spin City* (which ran from 2000 to 2002) before joining the cast of *Two and a Half Men* in the leading role. He has lived a notorious life, and has been making headlines for substance abuse and his turbulent domestic life ever since the late 1990s.

The pair seemed friendly at first, and Sheen even showed some admiration toward Chuck after a few seasons of *Two and a Half Men*: 'When you do research on him, you realise how prolific he is in the annals of TV history…So, you're expecting a much older guy when you walk in the room. When I first met him, I asked, "When did you start all this, when you were 18?" But throughout 2010 and into early 2011, Charlie once again got in trouble with his drug habit, and took a hiatus from filming the show to enter into rehab. Things escalated once Chuck Lorre complained about Charlie in a vanity card following *Two and a Half Men* (see the 'Vanity Card' entry), and Charlie then did a series of interviews revealing his views on his relationship with Chuck: 'It was a fake friendship…I never felt respected in a way that I should have been,' he told ABC's *20/20*. Charlie was eventually fired from the show on 7 March 2011, in a very acrimonious split. On 13 May 2011, it was announced that Ashton Kutcher would be taking over his place in the show.

At least Chuck had *The Big Bang Theory* to take refuge in, and his new television series *Mike & Molly*, both of which, for now, seem drama free. Maybe the answer to Chuck's woes is ensemble casts, with no single major star! Still, once the firestorm of publicity around *Two and a Half Men* dies down, Chuck is sure be able to take pleasure in the recognition he deserves – with three shows on the rise, there's no reason why he shouldn't be on top of the world.

Mann, Aarti

Aarti plays Priya Koothrappali, Rajesh's smart, beautiful sister and Leonard's girlfriend in the third season of the show. Her extended role on the show wasn't a guarantee, but her infectious energy helped her mesh with the rest of *The Big Bang Theory* stars: 'She did one episode this season, and we just really loved Aarti, and her work ethic kind of melded with everybody else's,' said Johnny Galecki (Leonard).

Her full name is Aarti Majmudar Mankad and she is sometimes credited in earlier roles as Aarti Majmudar. She attended the Tisch School of Arts in New York, a prestigious theatre school which has several well-known alumni like *The Big Bang Theory*'s Simon Helberg, Debra Messing (*Will & Grace*), Kristen Bell (*Veronica Mars*) and many more. She was the voice of the audio book for Kaavya Viswanathan's controversial debut novel *How Opal Mehta Got Kissed, Got Wild, and Got a Life*, which was eventually pulled from the shelves over allegations of plagiarism.

The Big Bang Theory is by far Aarti's most high-profile role to date, although we hope to see more of her soon.

Mommas (and Poppas)

If there are any scene-stealers in *The Big Bang Theory*, they are surely found in the incredible array of actresses playing the boys' mothers. From the booming voice of Carol Ann Susi, who plays Howard Wolowitz's off-camera mum, to Christine Baranski as Leonard's uber-critical psychologist mother, the mommas are set to rule the show whenever they appear.

Carol Ann Susi is one of those actresses you'd know if you saw her – she's been constantly on television screens for over twenty years in roles as diverse as *Cheers*, *That '70s Show* and *CSI*. Just don't expect to ever see her on *Big Bang Theory*! When asked about the reclusive Mrs. Wolowitz, who so far has only been heard shouting at her son from another room, Chuck Lorre said: 'It's a spectacular voice, isn't it?…I think [she's] best left to the imagination.' Luckily, Carol Ann doesn't seem to have a problem with it: 'I've always been an on-camera actress, so to suddenly be doing voice-over stuff is fabulous,' she told *TV Guide*. But that doesn't mean that she doesn't get recognised while out and about: 'I once got outed by a waitress while having dinner. She started screaming, "Oh, my God! How-ARD!" And I've even been outed by a bus driver. I don't drive. I live in L.A., but I take the bus. I know, I'm weird!' As for Howard's dad, who ran out on his family when Howard was only eleven, there is some speculation that he might show up on the show sometime. Simon Helberg has a very specific idea as to who should play his father, inspired by Howard's Beatles-esque hairstyle: 'I would like his father to be Ringo Starr. How cool would it be if Wolowitz is the son of a Beatle?' he laughed to *Entertainment Weekly*.

The whole cast were a bit star-struck when Christine Baranski was cast as Leonard's mom. Christine has a

THE BIG BANG THEORY A–Z

long history with Chuck Lorre that goes back to his
Cybill days, when Chuck's writing helped Christine to
pull in an Supporting Actress Emmy. Johnny Galecki
was worried that Christine was only coming in as a
favour to Chuck, and that she wouldn't generate the
same chemistry as the other guest stars. But instead,
they got pure professionalism, and having Christine on
set was a masterclass in sitcom acting to all the other
actors on set. 'She gets [here], and she knows every
episode and she's spending her lunch hours going over
her lines,' said Galecki to Bullz-Eye.com. 'You know,
she's not phoning anything in whatsoever.' Christine
was so good as Leonard's mom that she was nominated
for a 2009 Emmy in the 'Outstanding Guest Actress in
a Comedy Series' category. When they brought her
back the next year for another episode, she was
nominated for the Emmy again. Talk about an amazing
repeat performance!

As if that wasn't enough, another famous mom is
Laurie Metcalf, who plays Sheldon's God-fearing,
Texas mother with aplomb. Best known for her work
on *Roseanne*, and for recurring roles in *Desperate
Housewives* and *3rd Rock from the Sun*, Laurie is a stand-
out actress of modern comedy. 'Laurie, I'd take any
opportunity to work with. Laurie is one of the top

three most talented actresses alive right now. She's incredible,' said Johnny Galecki to *The A.V. Club*. Johnny would also love to see Laurie and Christine come together on set one day: 'I hope there is some holiday episode one year where, you know, Christmas at the Coopers or something like that would be pretty amazing,' he told Bullz-Eye.com. 'It's also great even when we're just riffing on sets to talk about who each character's parents would be. There's really no better insight into your character than meeting your character's parent. Just as it is in life. There's no better insight to your friend or spouse than spending time with one of their parents.'

With so much focus on the moms, it's clear there's a big gap on the father side of things. In fact, at the moment only Raj's father has played any role whatsoever in the show. Dr. V.M. Koothrappali is played by Brian George, who is a British-Israeli actor best known for playing characters of South Asian descent. Raj's mother (Mrs. Koothrappali) is portrayed by Alice Amter, a beautiful British-Indian actress. Despite (so far) only being shown on video chat on the show, Alice and Brian still sometimes come out to the live tapings to get some feedback from the audience, who show them the love! 'We do the bows, we take our curtain call at the end of the live studio taping. [The audience] seem to be very interested and involved when we're on; they seem to know who we are.' Alice really hopes that one day the Koothrappali parents will get to escape the screen and visit their son one day! 'There's a lot of talk about that,' said Alice to TVDoneWright.com. 'You know, one can only hope. …We've been there since Season 1, and we definitely feel part, Brian and I, of the core cast, so that's nice.'

Movie Versions

Many fans are wondering when there is going to be a movie version of *The Big Bang Theory*, following the success of other television shows that have made the jump (like *Sex and the City*). Kunal Nayyar, however, doesn't believe there will be one any time soon: 'Because of the format, multi-camera shot in front of a live audience, it would be very strange. No other sitcom in that form – *Friends, Seinfeld* – has ever done it before. I could see how single camera shows, such as *30 Rock* or *The Office*, could be a movie but because of the way we shoot I don't think so,' he said to *Metro*.

Mystic Warlords of Ka'a

Mystic Warlords of Ka'a is a fantasy card game invented specifically for *The Big Bang Theory*, in the tradition of collectible card games like Magic: The Gathering. It is played by the whole gang (with the exception of Penny, although she did give it a try once) and there are tournaments held in the Comic Center.

According to Wil Wheaton's blog, there isn't an actual card set yet of Mystic Warlords of Ka'a, but 'the show's art department made actual cards with actual graphics and rules on them, and we all spent a fair amount of time making up some logical rules to go with [it].' It just goes to show how much dedication the show's production put in to make everything realistic and logical.

NASA

It must take a lot to excite the scientists and engineers over at NASA about something happening down here on Earth, but a cameo of one of their inventions on the set of *The Big Bang Theory* is creating a massive buzz! The invention in question is an educational beach ball printed with data from the Wilkinson Microwave Anisotropy Probe (WMAP), and it sits on a shelf in Leonard and Sheldon's apartment. The team at NASA describe it on their blog: 'Imagine yourself at the center of this ball, looking in all directions. What you are seeing is the first visible light in the universe. It has been stretched by the very fabric of space/time as the universe has expanded so it now is microwave light, invisible to our eyes (but not WMAP's telescopes!).'

NASA contacted *The Big Bang Theory* to get a photo of the ball for use on their blog, and instead they were treated to an on-set tour. As a thank-you, the NASA team brought even more gadgets for the boys to have in their apartment, so watch out for even more NASA-related goodies on set in the future.

Nayyar, Kunal

Kunal Nayyar is one of only very few 'Indian Indians' working on a current American television series today. 'It's kind of historic, what's happening here…It's a pretty big deal,' he told *east-west* magazine. And although his character has one of the longest names in television (Rajesh Ramayan Koothrappali), Kunal finds *his* name is the more difficult to pronounce: 'Surprisingly my character's name rolls off the tongue pretty easily for everyone. It is my real name (Kunal) that sometimes is harder for the directors, producers, and writers and they have a harder time getting that out correct. I have heard

KUNAL NAYYAR (RAJESH KOOTHRAPPALI) WITH HIS PARENTS

some really fantastic versions of my name from them,'
he laughed to *ChitChat Girl*.

Kunal was born in London, England on 30 April
1981 but moved with his family to New Delhi, India,
when he was five. His mother worked as an interior
designer and his father is an accountant. While in high
school in New Delhi, he did some plays in high school,
but wasn't really sure it was a viable career. Luckily for
Kunal, his parents were fully supportive of him no
matter what he wanted to do. 'The circle that I grew
up in is very different from what you call a traditional
Indian family. My parents are like, "Yeah, go act!" and
all bohemian and they're smoking cigarettes, which is
something you very rarely see. That's maybe 10 percent
of India and the rest of it is very conservative.'

When he was 18 he decided to go to college in the
US. He chose the University of Portland in Oregon,
where he did a Bachelor of Science in Business
Administration. Outside of his classes, he was intrigued
by the acting scene, and got involved in his first proper
plays, hanging out with the local theatre-crowd. 'I took
all the acting classes and did all the plays but graduated
with my degree in business because I wanted
something to fall back on.' Yet the modest Kunal was in
fact highly praised as an actor during his undergraduate

career, and went on to win the Irene Ryan National Acting Award and Mark Twain National Award for Comedic Acting. He was also invited to attend the prestigious Sundance Theatre Lab workshop in Utah in 2003. His business degree wasn't a total waste though – he credits it with giving him the skills to better market himself in a difficult industry where actors are often taken advantage of.

Like his *The Big Bang Theory* coworker Jim Parsons, Kunal then went on to get a Masters of Fine Arts in acting, from Temple University in Philadelphia. 'I just fell in love with the entire art form [of theatre]. The thrill of being in front of an audience…they're breathing with you, they're laughing with you, they're crying with you, so that's a thrill I didn't get in any other field.' After his Masters finished in 2006, he starred in several acclaimed theatre productions. Not only did he win a Garland Award for Best Male Actor for his part in 'Huck and Holden' for the Dahlia Theatre in Los Angeles, but he went back to England to star in a well-received production of Shakespeare's 'Love's Labour's Lost' with the Royal Shakespeare Company in Stratford-Upon-Avon.

Through his acting agency Kunal was actively looking for television roles too, after deciding to broaden his résumé outside of just theatre. He got a guest appearance on *NCIS* ('it was fun because I got to play a terrorist and I am such the opposite of that which was great') but it wasn't long before the casting call for *The Big Bang Theory* came up. Kunal read the part of then 'David' Koothrappali and realised that this could be his big break. He knew how he wanted to play the part, and so he put on his thickest New Delhi accent (the kind he only normally has once he's hanging out with his friends back home in India) and nailed the audition.

Now, he feels absolutely blessed to have secured such a great role on a popular sitcom. He differs in many ways from Raj, but that doesn't lessen his enjoyment of playing him. 'I'm not a genius, I can talk to women without being drunk, I'm not shy and I'm very open. So in many ways I'm not like Raj, but playing him is wonderful because I get to see the world through very innocent eyes and that, for me, as an actor, is just a joy.'

It's also been fun for Kunal to see his success grow in his home country. Initially, the show was only aired on a cable channel in India, which had a comparatively small audience to the regular shows. It made him a celebrity in some circles but not in others, and even his family weren't sure what exactly he was involved with. That all changed when his mother flew over to Los Angeles to watch a taping – and ended up crying through the whole thing. 'She actually could not believe that this is how big it is,' said Kunal to *east-west* magazine. And now the popularity of the show has skyrocketed in India after it started to air on the English language Indian channel Zee Cafe: 'It's got tremendously big in the past year and it's gone insane. The show runs five times a week, four times a day so I don't know what it's going to be like the next time I go back to visit my parents in New Delhi.' As he now lives in Los Angeles full time, there are plenty of things he misses about India: 'I miss my parents, my cousins, my family. I miss Indian food, I miss chicken tikka masala – we call it butter chicken. They just don't make it the same in America. We've had the same cook at our house forever so I miss his cooking, too.' Kunal complained in an interview with *Divanee* about the food being offered on *The Big Bang Theory* set: 'they have egg whites and spinach downstairs. I'd rather have idlis for breakfast, dude.' (Idlis are a south Indian rice cake normally eaten for breakfast with chutney or other spiced sauces).

Kunal's big breakthrough as a non–stereotypical Indian character on American television has also helped to shepherd in a whole new crop of Indian actors onto the Hollywood scene. Kunal points out that although the show sometimes pokes fun at Indian culture, the show equally laughs at American culture – and they haven't pigeon-holed Raj as a taxi-driver or given him a turban to wear. Kunal thinks it's opened a lot of doors: 'This year [2010] a lot of the pilots that were shot and some that got picked up have had Indian characters. There's one called *Outsourced*, which NBC picked up, that is actually about a call centre in India and there's four Indian actors in that show, all of whom I know, obviously. We Indians always joke that we're the new black. The Indian community in America is getting bigger. It's a society that's very prevalent both financially as well as culturally. People have started to pay attention.'

Kunal is by no means resting on his laurels just because he's become part of a hit show. He wrote his own play called 'Cotton Candy', which became a massive hit in New Delhi. Writing is definitely something that Kunal would like to pursue in the future: 'I'd like to write my masterpiece one day. I have so many dreams but I have to make sure that I'm patient and I'm smart.' Yet his biggest dream is to return to his home country to act and also to encourage other Indian youngsters to pursue acting too: 'I dream of running an acting school in Delhi. I really want to do that. Besides this, I want to get into direction and production of films or shows.' Kunal has plenty of talent and, by the time *The Big Bang Theory* finishes, he will have plenty of experience too.

Nimoy Napkin

In the episode 'The Bath Item Gift Hypothesis' (Season 2, Episode 11), Penny gives Sheldon the best present he could ever imagine – the autograph and DNA of Leonard Nimoy. Leonard Nimoy played Spock in the original *Star Trek* series (1966–1969), and from that role has become one of the legendary actors in sci-fi history. Sheldon especially identifies with Spock, who, because of his half-Vulcan heritage, prefers to live by reason and logic rather than being ruled by emotion. Although the napkin used in the actual filming wasn't signed by Nimoy, the show sent him a napkin to sign for charity – along with an extra one in case he made a mistake. It turns out, that extra napkin was completely unnecessary: 'Only one came back signed,' said Jim Parsons to *TV Guide*. 'The other came back clean and clear; he's a pro!' The napkin was auctioned off at the The Beit T'Shuvah "Steps to Recovery" Gala for $1,100.

Star Trek legend Leonard Nimoy – the *Big Bang* creators would love to have him on the show!

For the cast, it would be a dream to have Leonard Nimoy appear on the show as a guest star. 'I think it would be amazing to have Leonard Nimoy, obviously because of the napkin. Anybody from *Star Wars*, *Star Trek*. They're like religions to these guys,' said Simon Helberg to *TVGuide Online*. Bill Prady would love it too, but he thinks it is unlikely. 'I don't think that there are any plans for that,' he told Alice Jester at a Comic-Con 2009 panel. 'It would be lovely. I know he doesn't do a lot of TV. He did that round on *Fringe*, I guess he got to be friends with JJ [Abrams] during the making of the *Star Trek* movie. I don't know, I think if he actually showed up on the show our characters' heads would explode. It might be the end of everything.'

Still, considering he has done guest spots for other shows, like *The Simpsons* and the aforementioned *Fringe*, there's a chance it might happen one day! *The Big Bang Theory* producers are keen not to simply stunt-cast, however. They like to have a proper story line for their guests and a real reason for them to appear: 'They're very smart about who they put on and how they do it. It's cool that more people are watching and now people want to do it. Those geeky icons are fans of the show and they want to come on and make fun of themselves,' continued Simon. Judging by how well other guests, like Stan Lee and Nobel Laureate George Smoot have been integrated into the series, the writer's are bound to find a clever way to fit in Nimoy, if he was willing!

0

The Observed Photon (and other T-shirts)

How many sitcoms can claim to have their own line of T-shirts? *The Big Bang Theory* can! There are so many classic lines from the show that work perfectly emblazoned across a tee – from the lyrics of 'Soft Kitty' to Sheldon's catchphrase 'Bazinga!' Yet the Observed Photon (the phenomenon demonstrated using the double-slit experiment, by which a photon changes its actions based on whether it is being watched or not) is unique in that it was Sheldon himself who thought it would make a great (albeit incredibly nerdy) line for a T-Shirt! The T-Shirts have been incredibly popular: 'These types of hot ticket *The Big Bang Theory* T-shirts are fast sellers, and we are even having trouble keeping them in stock because they literally fly off the shelves whenever we get them in,' said Fred Hajjar, Founder and CEO of www.TVStoreOnline.com. Why not check it out and see if you can get your own *Big Bang Theory* t-shirt to show off your love to the world!

On Set

With all the young, up-and-coming actors on set, there's bound to be chemistry – and sometimes it's not the good kind. Luckily for *The Big Bang Theory*, the cast (and crew) all get along really well, and love the work they do together. It's a big contrast to all the drama that Chuck has had to face on the sets of some of his other shows, that's for sure! Rather than being at each other's throats all the time and leaving their associations with each other at the studio, *The Big Bang Theory* cast play games together (their favourites being Scrabble and ping pong), arrange to meet for dinner at least once a week, and even go on holiday together.

During the live tapings, the cast are incredibly

professional. They have to be – they only have a very limited time to get an episode shot and ready to air. It means that the cast don't tend to mess around with the scripts that they get, despite some of them being accomplished improvisers. Kunal Nayyar told the *New York Post*: 'our tapings are so tight, we have it down to a real science. Plus, a lot of the language on the show is so specific that if you change a word it will mess up the whole speech rhythm.' That doesn't mean that they don't have fun on the set, however! Kunal is especially notorious for 'breaking' during a scene; in other words, he quite often can't control himself and starts to laugh at the show's jokes! 'I break all the time,' he continued to the *New York Post*. 'It's my own jokes [that make me laugh], actually, which is what makes it so sadly pretentious. I have a lot of one-liners and if the audience really laughs at one, I just can't keep it together. I know it sounds so lame to laugh at your own jokes.' It's not that lame when you think about all the hilarity they have to face, and Kunal is definitely one of the least experienced comic actors on set. He's not the only one to crack-up during takes either: 'we all break from time to time,' said Simon Helberg to *TV Guide*.

Kunal doesn't have to worry about his colleagues

getting frustrated with him, as they all help each other out. There is very little animosity on set (apart from around the ping pong table). Johnny Galecki spoke openly with the *LA Times* about the camaraderie on set: 'You don't have to be friends with your colleagues. But it all happened very naturally. The good thing is we allow ourselves our bad moods and dark days. There's no expectation to be buddy-buddy either. We're all kind of bracing for the day when we disappoint each other, anger each other, or get under someone's skin because so far we've just had so much fun.' For Johnny and Jim Parsons, the friendship actually was a bit forced to begin with – in a way, once they were cast, they felt like they had to spend some time together in order to make it appear more natural on screen. But luckily, instead of being a chore, it was great for both of them: 'After [we knew we were on the show], we spent some time together. Once we knew that we were gonna go forward, which I think a lot of actors try to do when your characters have a history together, to kind of do some accelerated bonding as much as you can before you get there and put it on film,' said Johnny to *The Culture Shock*.

The cast know just how rare it is to have such a great and easy bond, and don't take anything for granted. 'It's one of the luckiest things,' said Simon Helberg to the *LA Times*. 'We have a shorthand with each other. There's no tension. There's just honesty, and it doesn't feel competitive.'

For Bill Prady, it's an unreal experience. 'This is the best place I've ever worked,' he told the audiences at Comic-Con 2009. 'For a long time I said working with the Muppets and for a long time I said that was the best place I ever worked. Working with Jim Henson would never be topped and then I got here. You cannot top this cast and these people and it is true, true joy.'

Original Pilot

In 2006, a year before this current hit incarnation, Lorre had attempted an earlier *Big Bang* pilot called 'Lenny, Penny and Kenny'. This first attempt was a flop for many reasons, and even Lorre said that he knew it was not good: 'The first pilot we wrote for the show was wrong. I don't know any other word to use for it.' (*Watch!* magazine). This original pilot still featured Johnny Galecki as Leonard and Jim Parsons as Sheldon, which proves that it takes more than just brilliant actors to make a show.

The main problem with the original pilot was that it

lacked heart. The main female character of the show was named Katie – an aspiring actress who was much more street-smart and fierce than the current main female lead, Penny. The idea was that the two nerdy boys would eventually break down her hard shell and she would develop into a sweeter character. This meant that initially she didn't treat the two geeks across the hall as nicely as Penny did, and was much more sarcastic and sassy. It didn't go down well. The show's male characters were so innocent in their geekdom that the audience became protective of them. And so when 'Katie' acted more manipulative with these malleable men, 'it was like she was shooting fish in a barrel. It didn't work,' Galecki told *Watch!* magazine. 'We've had that problem with guest stars too,' the actor notes. 'If they're too malicious towards the guys or show too much of an edge, the audience hates them.'

The original Katie was portrayed by the Canadian actress Amanda Walsh, who is best known in her native country for being a *MuchMusic* VJ. Unfortunately, Chuck and Bill knew she wouldn't be right for the rewritten version of her character, as they were now aiming for someone younger and more innocent looking – hence why Kaley Cuoco was called back.

The original pilot also didn't feature Howard and Raj;

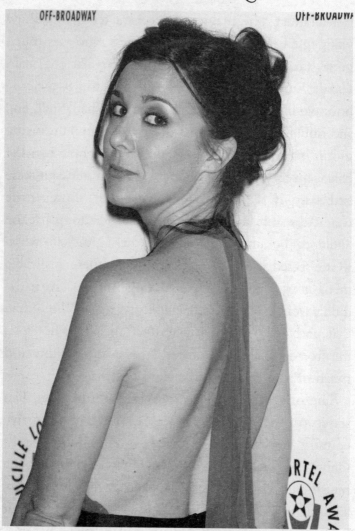

IRIS BAHR, WHO APPEARED IN THE ORIGINAL PILOT EPISODE OF
THE BIG BANG THEORY

instead, there was a very nerdy female character named Gilda in the group instead, played by Iris Bahr, who has guest-starred in many sitcoms like *Friends*, *The Drew Carey Show* and *The King of Queens*, as well as playing the lead role in *Larry the Cable Guy: Health Inspector*. Chuck and Bill quickly realised that they wanted to increase the group size and give Sheldon and Leonard other characters to play off of: 'The idea was, if they like these first two guys, let's give them two more. I also like the way Wolowitz and Koothrappali "bracket" Leonard and Sheldon by being more withdrawn [Koothrappali] and more socially confident – albeit in a deluded way [Wolowitz],' said Bill to *Variety*. It also didn't have the catchy Barenaked Ladies theme song, but used the Thomas Dolby hit 'She Blinded Me With Science'. They did have Dr. Saltzberg still – their science consultant! But for the original pilot, they went a little too far into trying to portray a realistic working scientists' life: 'The set decorators visited my graduate students' apartments to get an idea of how physicists live. In the end, they used those ideas for a pilot, but people thought it was a little – depressing, I think? So they made a new pilot. The characters now live in a place that doesn't look anything like where my students live!' Saltzberg laughed to *UCLA Today*.

It's actually very rare in the television industry that a pilot ever gets a 'second chance', even if the concept is brilliant. But this was where Chuck's incredible reputation for creating hits really came to the fore: the network could see his enthusiasm for the project, and wanted to give Chuck the opportunity to get it right and really see his vision come to life. 'You either hear yes or no, you never hear, "Give it another shot." So that was CBS standing behind us,' said Johnny Galecki, on just how lucky he was to get another chance. Both Chuck and Bill knew they only had one more shot to nail it, and luckily they did!

P

Parsons, Jim

James Joseph 'Jim' Parsons is considered the breakout star of *The Big Bang Theory*. Not only has he been blessed by the critics, but he is appreciated by the acting academies, who shower him with awards, and with the fans, amongst whom he has an almost cult-like following. But it almost wasn't to be…if Jim had had his way, he might have only studied acting, rather than making acting history himself.

Jim was born on 24 March, 1973 in Houston, Texas (not such a far cry from his character, Sheldon, who is

JIM PARSONS, WHO PLAYS DR. SHELDON COOPER, SIGNING AUTOGRAPHS FOR *BIG BANG THEORY* FANS

also a Texas boy!) to elementary school teacher mother Judy, and his dad Mickey, who was president of a plumbing company. He has one younger sister, called Julie. Ever since playing a Kola-Kola bird in an elementary school production of 'The Elephant Child' at only six years old, complete with yellow tights and a feathered breastplate, Jim fell in love with acting and performing. 'I don't know that I was good…but I obviously caught a bug.' He might not have been good, but the small role certainly had an impact on him – he remembers his Kola-Kola bird song to this day and sang it in an interview after he won his Emmy.

He continued to try out for school plays throughout his high school career at Klein Oak High School in Spring, Texas, including parts in 'Wait Until Dark' (which his sister, Julie, also had a role in) and 'Unseen Noises'. His drama teacher, Margaret Locher, called Jim 'the funniest person I've ever known…He's one of those people that when he's onstage, he lights up the entire stage – it's hard to watch anybody else because Jim occupies the entire stage,' she said to *Entertainment Tonight*.

After finishing high school in 1991, he started university at the University of Houston for a three-year undergraduate degree. Interestingly, his time as an undergraduate was the only time Jim thought about a possible back-up plan in case acting didn't work out for him. His second choice of career? Being a weatherman! 'When I was in college, I had to take a science class, and I thought, well, you love hurricanes. I loved the drama of it.' Unfortunately, it didn't quite go as planned for Jim, who – it turns out – wasn't cut out for the rigours of science. 'There was a lot going on in my life then, and I would show up to class and be shocked that they were taking a test. I couldn't believe it. They'd bring out calculators, and I thought, what do we need a calculator for? And I failed. It was the only F I ever got.' 'It turns out, the sciences didn't want me any more than I wanted them,' he continued to *Watch!* magazine. Not yet at least!

It isn't a surprise that Jim was sometimes too busy to pay attention in class – he was acting almost non-stop. He starred in the 1994 University of Houston production of Tom Stoppard's *Rosencrantz and Guildenstern are Dead*, where his performance as Rosencrantz was praised in the *Houston Press*: 'James Parsons and Matthew Carter possess their roles with an easy presence and a deft wit – the stage is theirs. Their timing is almost always impeccable – an important issue, given that *Rosencrantz and Guildenstern Are Dead* is a timing play. The swashbuckling word play could easily become tiresome. But that doesn't happen with Parsons and Carter. We eat it up and want more.' Jim also went on to help establish an independent theatre company in Houston called Infernal Bridegroom Productions (IBP), and starred in eighteen of their productions including 'Endgame' by Samuel Beckett, 'Guys and Dolls' by Frank Loesser and 'Abe Burrows' and 'Camino Real' by Tennessee Williams, and was labeled 'one of the troupe's most talented actors' by the *Houston Press*. Whereas his undergraduate studies (and later his graduate school experience) focused on traditional acting and stage work, the work he did IBP was much more off-beat and modern, with plays performed in warehouses and parking lots or wherever the actors could find some space. 'There were a lot of important lessons that I learned [from IBP], including the ability to perform under any circumstances. You can only learn it by getting the chance to do it, to perform in whatever room, in front of whatever audience that you have.' When he wasn't on stage with IBP, he was acting for the Stages Repertory Theatre, which the *Houston Chronicle* calls 'Houston's off-Broadway'.

By the end of his undergrad degree, Jim was ready to move away from Texas. He felt like he had exhausted all the theatre opportunities that Houston had to offer. But

Jim wasn't quite ready to try New York or Los Angeles just yet. 'I'm brave, but I'm not that brave,' he laughed to the *Playbill*. 'So I thought, you know, grad school would be a wonderful thing, not only an excuse to get out of town, but a useful thing for me to do... And I remember very distinctly making some sort of conscious decision to go ahead and share with people [that] I was auditioning for grad schools and that I really wanted to do this. It was one of the first examples in my life when I realised that if you really put it out there and tell everybody that you want something, you magnify for yourself how important it is, which probably makes you work that much harder at it.'

His hard work paid off, and he was accepted into a very prestigious two-year training course in classical theatre at the University of San Diego (in conjunction with the Old Globe Theatre), which only accepts seven students a year. Jim credits the program with helping him to break down Sheldon's complex dialogue, in a similar way that Jim was taught to do for Shakespeare in his graduate school days. 'I cannot say, and I mean this quite sincerely, how often my time at grad school at USD enters my mind...The type of work I did in that program to get through some of those Shakespearean texts is very similar to the work strategy

I use to get through these scientifically dense speeches I have to get through now,' he told the *San Diego Union Tribune*. Jim loved school, and the study of theatre. In 2001, Jim graduated with a Masters of Fine Arts in Dramatic Arts, and he moved to New York to find acting work, but in some ways it was only because he couldn't continue studying his craft. He told *Newsweek* that, 'If they offered a doctorate in acting, I'd still be there. It was so safe! I went to grad school. I kept going as long as they'd have me.' (Love of academia – yet another thing that Jim has in common with Sheldon – although Sheldon most likely would not approve of Jim's choice of doctorate, it's far too soft!)

Yet in 2001, just before his graduation, tragedy struck Jim and his family, as his father was killed in a car accident. It affected Jim deeply, as he had always been close to his father, who had supported him completely in his dream to be an actor. 'It changed the whole family dynamic,' he told *Pop Matters*. 'When I went home after that I still hadn't graduated. I had a final project and I know they told me, "You don't have to come back right away". It was very interesting that I knew I had to go back and do that because whether or not you could be of use at home – I realised in the end I could only be of use to the family fully if I did what

I needed to do and then went on… What's funny is I then moved to New York and [normally I] have a terrible sense of direction – my dad was very good at it – and I understood the city and how to get around so quickly that it boggled my mind. And still, to this day, I think it had something to do with [his death].'

New York was moderately successful for Jim. He starred in a few off-Broadway productions and television commercials. His most famous commercial was for the toasted sandwich chain Quiznos, which controversially depicted Jim as a man raised by wolves who still suckled his wolf-mother's milk! Some of his other roles were equally off-beat, including his turn as Tim in the Zach Braff movie *Garden State* (2004). Tim was an armour-wearing, Klingon-speaking, knight-in-training, which means that Sheldon isn't the first of Jim's characters to speak the *Star Trek* language. Jim finds his predisposition to playing geeky characters quite funny, as he is not a sci-fi geek himself at all: 'Who knows why somebody who has never watched *Star Trek* – who had no idea what the Klingon language would sound like – has been asked twice in his adult life to play somebody who has an intimate relationship with this Klingon language. But, and this is an easy example, why would somebody who's asked to [agree to] play a murderer? What fits naturally about that? What looks right? Yes, he could kill someone?'

More bit parts in movies followed, in films such as *Heights* (2005) and *10 Items or Less* (2006), but his biggest job was in the television series *Judging Amy*. Jim featured in seven episodes from 2004–2005 as Rob Holbrook, a young clerk whose Spanish-speaking skills come in handy during a trial. Yet all the while, Jim was audition for pilots for television shows that were never picked up by the networks. In total, he auditioned for over 16 pilots, for show like *Blitt Happens* directed by the Farrelly brothers (*There's Something about Mary*, *Dumb & Dumber*) and *Taste* by Jane Krakowski before getting the news about *The Big Bang Theory*.

When Jim first received *The Big Bang Theory* script in early 2007 and read the part of Sheldon, he instantly felt a connection – not with the character, but with the language. 'As a character, I don't know I felt a relation at all. What I had a feeling about was the way the dialogue was structured, the way they had structured Sheldon's speeches. Sheldon has always taken that many words to get to a point. I thought, and I still think, they brilliantly use those words that most of us don't recognize to create that rhythm. And the rhythm got me. It was the chance to dance through that dialogue, and in a lot of ways still is.' It was the height of Oscar season, and Jim steadfastly refused to go to any of the parties or events so he could stay at home and memorise his Sheldon lines. He knew he would just kick himself if he didn't throw everything he had at trying to get this part, because he knew deep down that this was his role. 'I was specifically excited about the pilot for *Big Bang*, because when you go in for sixteen pilots, and you've done that for a few years in a row, you very quickly realise that there may be a lot of parts you can play, but the ones that you match up with really well are pretty rare,' he said to *Playbill*. In the end, he blew Chuck Lorre and Bill Prady away with his audition, and got the job. 'I did jump up and down when I got this part, which is not my normal reaction to things.'

It's no understatement to say that Sheldon has changed Jim's life forever. Not only has the role brought him critical acclaim and financial success, but it has catapulted Jim into cult status amongst the fans. Everything from his favourite sayings, to the T-shirts he wears are copied and revered throughout the fandom. He has become a geek icon, even if he shares little of his character's interests in real life. 'His interests are so divergent from mine,' said Jim to *USA Today*. 'I don't know comic books at all. I don't know superheroes at all, unless they're out in movies.' Instead, Jim loves to debate politics while watching *The McLaughlin Group* (a weekly public affairs show). Still, Jim is Sheldon in the eyes of fans, and even Jim concedes that there are some similarities: 'I've got some grumpy-old-man aspects of me, [but] I'm not nearly as rigid as Sheldon,' continued Jim. 'I can be a little obsessive with things, but not quite to the degree he can.' What kinds of things is Jim obsessive about? 'I like words, and I like numbers. I like crossword puzzles a lot. I like to deal with lists and rankings and statistics. I'm surprised I'm not more into baseball, because I could geek on that. I love "Casey Kasem's Top 40", I love that order. I love seeing what were the nominated Oscar films.'

One thing that Jim doesn't have to worry about now is finding extra work. With *The Big Bang Theory* set to continue into the 2013–2014 season, he can be comfortable that he will be on our screens for a long time. In fact, *The Big Bang Theory* was so dominant in his mind that for the first few hiatuses (i.e. when the sitcom takes a break for the summer and there is no filming going on), Jim didn't actively look for work. 'It's been hard to get mentally specific about [what I want to do], because you get so wrapped up in the show that

it's hard to go, "What I really want to do is blah blah blah." I don't find that I have the mental room for that.'

In 2011, however, Jim felt that familiar itch to return to theatre. 'Doing live theatre has been such a part of my life for all of my adult years...And I think that it was only going to be a matter of time before it reared its ugly head – that need to want to do theatre again,' he told *Playbill*. And so he joined the cast of director Joel Grey's Broadway production of Larry Kramer's 'The Normal Heart'. The show opened on 27 April 2011, and depicts a group of gay men living New York in the early 1980s, dealing with the early horrors of the AIDS epidemic.

Whatever Jim does now, he's bound to find success follows. And even now, his attitude is to work as hard as he can, with the faith that that work will lead him where he is meant to be: 'You just pour yourself into it, and it'll lead to something else. Whenever this road ends, or even during this trip as we're going down it, I will do other things.' For now though, we're glad he's committed to doing *The Big Bang Theory*, and look forward to see him bringing Sheldon to life for years to come.

OPPOSITE: JIM PARSONS HAS WON A HOST OF AWARDS FOR HIS ROLE AS SHELDON COOPER

Penelope 'Penny'

When Penny moves in across the hall, Leonard can't believe his luck – and Sheldon can't see the appeal. At first, she appears just like the typical girl-next-door: ditzy, dim but with a good heart. But the more the boys learn about Penny, the more complex she becomes; it's clear she's more than just a wannabe actress. Her skills might be different from the boys' (she might not be a PhD in theoretical physics, for example!) but she does have her own knowledge bank that the boys couldn't possibly replicate: 'She grew up on a farm,' explained Chuck Lorre to *Deseret News*. 'She can fix a tractor. She can birth a calf, and she can do just about damn near anything that these guys can just sit around and talk about…She's an extraordinary character in her own right, but in a different world than theirs.' As Jim Parsons later pointed out to *Deseret News*, Penny has 'barn smarts' as opposed to 'book smarts'.

Penny gained all of her 'barn smarts' from her hometown of Omaha, Nebraska. Her last name hasn't been revealed on the show yet. She's pretty, outgoing and popular, but still struggles with achieving her dream. She is the ordinary girl attempting to find her place in the world, and in that way, her character is probably the most relatable of all the five main cast.

PENNY, WHO LIVES ACROSS THE HALL FROM LEONARD AND SHELDON,
IS PLAYED BY KALEY CUOCO

Kaley Cuoco, who plays her on the show, understands this perfectly. She said to *IGN*: '[Penny's] definitely not perfect…She's a real girl. She's smart in her own way, and I think I represent the audience – like I'm looking at [the other characters] through [the audience's] eyes, because they are so different than what we are all used to… But she has totally grown. And like Chuck said, she has a lot of her own baggage. She wants to do things. She doesn't want to waitress for the rest of her life, and she has struggles every single day.'

Kaley loves the way the fans have embraced her character: 'The nerds are coming out of the closet. I'm not going to lie. They've become obsessed with the show. I think they love my character because she's so sweet with the guys on the show. She's slowly becoming one of them. She's accepted as one of them, and she's not judgemental. Penny is just such a loveable character.' Hopefully as the seasons progress, we will learn a lot more about Penny and her background – and maybe see her gain some success as an actress herself!

Ping Pong

So what do you get when you mix a bunch of young actors, one almost-professional athlete and a lot of

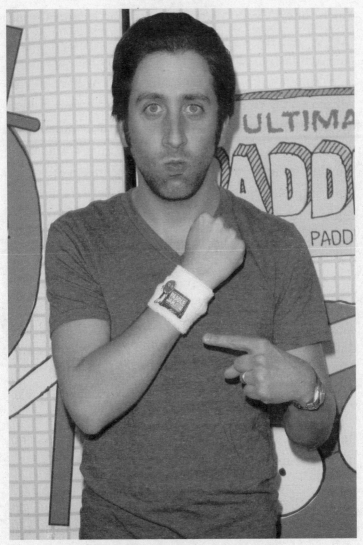

Simon Helberg at a celebrity ping pong tournament

down time? A very competitive set! The gang really get their competitive juices flowing by battling it out at table tennis. There are normally three tables on the set at all times – although sometimes the cast have to run around trying to find out where they have been folded up and hidden away. Kaley Cuoco has the reputation as the best player – but that's hardly surprising considering she almost chose to play professional tennis over acting! Jim, Simon and Kunal are all getting better though and ready to challenge Kaley over the title. And they have plenty of chances: 'All the crew, we play ping pong all day long. We have tournaments, trophies there,' Kaley said to *Delco* magazine. Kunal Nayyar got particularly upset when ping pong was brought up at Comic-Con 2009 – he gets stuck in to the on-set tournaments and this time he didn't do so well: 'I don't want to talk about it. Just had a tough defeat in the tournament… And, then Kaley comes in wearing short, sexy clothes to like mess with us. So this year in the tournament, I wore short, sexy clothes.' Needless to say, that distraction technique didn't work particularly well for Kunal!

The only person with zero interest in participating is Johnny Galecki (maybe because he's scared to get beaten by Kaley!) His reasons? 'I just have no interest. If you were to watch these games, you would understand how cutthroat they are. [The participating cast and crew] are so nasty towards one another. They're just terrible. They're awful. I don't want to be a part of it at all,' he told *Movieline*. 'Knock a little ball around? I'd rather sleep. Come to set and you'll understand. Although you'll probably be fascinated by the violence in it all but then you'd get tired and want a nap too.'

Johnny has to get used to it though – Kaley confessed to *Delco* mag that ping pong has become such a big part of their *Big Bang Theory* lives that Chuck Lorre might just write it into the script one day!

Prady, Bill

Bill Prady has taken his geekiest instincts and turned them into gold. Without his experience – and his memories of extremely nerdy friends – there would be no *Big Bang Theory*. Parts of Bill's life inform each one of the characters, from knowing someone in real life exactly like Sheldon to feeling a bit like Leonard himself sometimes: a nerd-at-heart who just wishes he could fit in sometimes. '[There's a] part of me that says…gee, I wish I could be one of those people who can just go to parties, and that's Leonard,' said Bill – although now that he's constantly at awards shows and

BILL PRADY, CO-CREATOR OF *THE BIG BANG THEORY*

cast parties, he probably feels a lot less like Leonard after all!

Bill was born on 7 June 1960 in Detroit, Michigan, and he didn't fall into his writing career immediately. After dropping out of college at Wayne State University in Michigan, he started work at Radio Shack (a computer parts/electronics store) and owned a share in a software company called The Small Computer Company as a self-taught computer programmer. It was there that he met many of the friends and colleagues who would become his inspiration for characters and dialogue on *The Big Bang Theory*.

Computer programming wasn't for him, and he sold up his shares and went to work for Jim Henson and the Muppets. He took to television writing immediately, and after scripting several shows like *Jim Henson Hour*, *Fraggle Rock* and *Walt Disney World's Muppet Vision 3D*, Bill jumped to writing sitcoms. He wrote for *Married…With Children* as a freelancer before eventually being hired onto the *Dharma & Greg* team.

Of course, not every sitcom that a writer works on can be a huge success, and after a string of hits Bill Prady found himself at a bit of a loose end, producing the teen drama *Gilmore Girls* and writing for a sitcom called *Related* by the former producer of *Friends*, Marta

Kauffman. Neither project was working particularly well for him, nor did he really enjoy what he was doing at the time, and so he decided to call up his friend Chuck Lorre to find out if he was working on something more interesting. Chuck was actually developing a sci-fi novel at the time, but together they quickly realised it was a bad plan: 'After a month, Chuck realised we couldn't do it. Just for the record, I realised it after three weeks,' he said to *Variety*.

It was then that Bill brought his idea about computer programmers to the table, and *The Big Bang Theory* was born. Currently, Bill's life is dedicated to all things *Big Bang* related, which suits him just fine!

Props

Want to know just how dedicated a show is to its concept? Just take a quick look at their set! For *The Big Bang Theory*, it is clear that a lot of care and attention goes into making Sheldon and Leonard's apartment (and other sets) feel just right – even down to the details that will never get picked up by a television camera.

The amazing props are mostly chosen by set decorator Ann Shea. Ann has worked on many shows before *Big Bang Theory*, but never one that was quite so challenging (and fun!) to decorate appropriately! Every item on the set is chosen for its authenticity and context – would a pair of nerdy physicists really have that item in their home? And the set also caters to Sheldon's neuroses – the cereals are always in the perfect place and everything is labelled, even if you would never be able to see the labels on screen. When Maria Montoya of *The Times-Picayune* went to visit the set, she described some of the amazing little touches that she noticed: 'Drawers in the piece were labelled "Luke", "Vader", "Solo" and even "Lamb Chop" – all telling details, but so tiny the camera would never know them.' They also try to make it feel like a real, working apartment. For example, they change the cereal brands every week 'to make it seem like people are really living there,' said Shea. She also picked out many shelves' worth of science books that she thought the boys would own, often with fun titles like *Inner Space, Outer Space* by David Schramm and *Moscow Twilight* by William E. Holland.

Ann spent several weeks trawling through old sets of sci-fi movies and junkyards to find the eclectic mix of objects in the boys' apartment. There is an astronomical globe, a telescope, old rocket parts from a Los Angeles

Aerospace junkyard, a pressure gauge and a handheld radiation detector, among others. When asked by *EW* about her methods, Shea said: 'I just picked out things that looked interesting.'

Some of these 'interesting' objects didn't come cheap, like the stuff from the junkyard! The six-foot-tall sculpture of DNA sequences, which was built out of two smaller versions and stands as a prominent feature of the boys' living room – cost almost $4,000. Somehow it is doubtful that two young scientists would be able to afford the sculpture in real life, but it is also likely that the two built it themselves! Even the time machine, for which the gang pooled together $800 for in Season 1, Episode 14, 'The Nerdvana Annihilation', was an actual replica version from the film that cost $50,000 to build in real life. It even came with its own bodyguard. Kunal Nayyar (Raj) was amazed. 'I'm like [to the bodyguard], "This is your job?" This is what he said: "This is your job, this is my job." [I responded:] "Cool. I didn't mean to offend you, I was just seriously asking.'

It's not all work and no play for the boys and there are plenty of sci-fi toys around to distract them! From the Green Lantern's lantern to a Batman cookie jar, there's lots of fun stuff to sit alongside the science. In fact, that's

Johnny Galecki's favourite part of the set: 'I like all of the figurines,' he said to *IGN*. 'The craftsmanship of some of these things is really incredible.'

It also helps that DC Comics has an office on the Warner Brothers lot. 'We called them up and said, "Can our set dresser come over and get some stuff?",' said Bill Prady at the Comic Con Round Table. 'They sent us boxes and boxes of stuff to put on the set, so most of it is in our offices.'

Penny's apartment has its own special prop-needs too: magazines, and lots of them! They tend to be of the trashy celebrity variety, especially *People* magazine. That's fine for Kaley Cuoco, as she needs something to read in the down time between takes: 'I've read every word of every page', she told *Delco* magazine.

Q

Quantum Physics

Quantum physics is one of the most complex branches of physics, which makes it a very appropriate study subject by our resident geeks! Quantum physics (which can also be known as quantum theory or quantum mechanics) attempts to study the behavior of the very smallest units that make up our universe – even smaller than atoms, called 'quanta' – and how this very tiny matter interacts with energy. Quantum physicist John Wheeler (see 'Whiteboards' to discover a hidden tribute to John Wheeler in the show) once famously said, 'If you are not completely confused by quantum mechanics, you do not understand it.'

By having the two main characters specialize in different areas of quantum physics, often considered one of the most difficult branch of physics to conceptualize, it enabled Chuck and Bill to develop the characters as intelligent beings without resorting to the normal 'nerd' characteristics: 'They're not entrepreneurs. They're scientists. That freed us up from a lot of clichés. No pocket protectors!' There was also no need for them to stare at computer screens all day – in fact, whiteboards are more important to quantum physicists, and 'we realised this was a better way to show somebody working with their mind,' said Bill Prady to *Science*, and the whiteboards also offered more opportunity for physical comedy (always important, especially with such great physical actors as Jim Parsons!). These boys have the brains to back up their nerdiness – which sets them apart from a lot of the other TV nerds out there.

R

Ratings

The Big Bang Theory was by no means an overnight success in the US. After good initial ratings for the pilot of 9.57 million viewers, it averaged 8 million viewers throughout its shortened first season. Those were respectable numbers for a new comedy, but far from a runaway hit.

But something remarkable happened in the second season: the ratings just kept on rising. The show moved time-slots to Monday evening at 8pm, and viewership hit 11 million viewers an episode by Christmas 2008. Chuck Lorre might have been at a loss to explain the rise, but Simon Helberg said: 'Maybe after a year of being on people are like, "Oh it's still on? Maybe it's worth checking out,"' he laughed to *The Boston Globe*. In its third season, it reached a milestone by overtaking *Two and a Half Men* in the particularly lucrative 25–54 demographic.

By the fourth season, *The Big Bang Theory* was the US's highest rated comedy overall, beating *Two and a Half Men* completely. Now, for Lorre, it's all about keeping things fresh: 'The magic trick of it all is, how do you keep it fresh without being redundant, without becoming a formulaic show where the audience is way ahead of you?' he asked in the *Brisbane Times*. Chuck has never had any trouble before, so we think this question is pretty rhetorical!

Rauch, Melissa

The Big Bang Theory is Melissa's first big recurring role on the small screen acting scene – but she's had her fair share of success already. Born on 23 June, 1980 in Marlboro, New Jersey (the same town as *The Vampire Diaries* star Paul Wesley), Melissa Ivy Rauch studied acting at Marymount Manhattan College in New York before going on to earn plaudits as a stand-up comedienne

MELISSA RAUCH, WHO PLAYS BERNADETTE ROSTENKOWSKI

in New York City. After her one-woman show, *Miss Education of Jenna Bush*, became a critical success in 2005, *Backstage* magazine wrote that she is 'a strong example of a comic who creates fun material for smart audiences, her dead-on observations about our pop culture and human foibles are the right mix of smart and silly…[she] will have you laughing and cheering'.

Her on-screen success ranges from big blockbuster movies like *I Love You, Man* to TV movies (*Wright vs Wrong*) and HBO shows, such as *True Blood*. She now plays Bernadette Rostenkowski, who has a PhD in microbiology, is Howard's on-off girlfriend (and now fiancée), and Penny's co-worker at the Cheesecake Factory. She's having great fun embodying Bernadette, but laughs at the paradox in her life: 'I'm so far from a science person… my science teachers are saying "bull-crap" [at the idea of her being a microbiologist],' she told Craig Ferguson on *The Late Late Show*.

Roseanne

Roseanne was a huge hit sitcom of the 1990s, and many of the *Big Bang* actors got their big break on that show. Chuck Lorre was a writer on the show, and Johnny Galecki, Sara Gilbert, Christine Baranski were all actors on the show. For Johnny and Sara, who started out played teenagers in love on the show, audiences got to watch them grow up on screen. In a lot of ways, they were more famous even than the big movie stars of the time, as their characters appeared on television sets in people's homes almost every night. Johnny remembers one time when he was out playing petanque with his friend at the time, Brad Pitt, 'and people would come up and touch me, because I was on TV. Meanwhile, Brad was on the side of every bus and on every billboard for his movie *Interview with the Vampire*. And he would say sarcastically, "Yeah, feel free to touch him."' he told *Watch!* magazine.

Even some of the actors not associated with Roseanne in a professional way were big fans of the show. Simon Helberg was one. In fact, had he met Johnny Galecki in his *Roseanne* days, he would have been really starstruck, as Johnny's character, David Healy had been one of his idols: "I always remember thinking he was really cool on *Roseanne*. I related a lot to his character… I always thought he had such cool hair. It was always, like, curly, in his face. And I was like, 'Man, I wish I had that curly, cool hair.' … And I recently – like right after I met [Johnny Galecki], I found this thing from when I was, like, 11 that I had to list my five favorite shows. And *Roseanne* was number one. So it is surreal,' Simon told CTV.ca.

Rostenkowski, Bernadette

Bernadette Maryann Rostenkowski starts out life on *The Big Bang Theory* as a graduate student studying microbiology, who is paying her way through school by working part-time at the Cheesecake Factory. Her job leads to her to meeting Penny, who then introduces her to Howard.

Bernadette and Howard get off to a rocky start, although they do eventually sustain a long-term relationship, and she even agrees to marry him! Bernadette is played by Melissa Rauch.

S

Saltzberg, David: Science expert

There is no way that *The Big Bang Theory* would be the show it is today without its resident astrophysicist, David Saltzberg. 'I can't overestimate his value to what we do,' said Bill Prady to *Science* magazine, and it's easy to see why.

David Saltzberg had no prior experience in television before joining *The Big Bang Theory*. He graduated from Princeton University in 1989 with a bachelor's degree in Physics, before gaining his PhD from the University of Chicago in 1994. He started work at UCLA in 1997 as a faculty member, before rising through the ranks to become a Professor.

Professor Saltzberg heard about *The Big Bang Theory* gig through a Hawaiian astrophysicist friend who had worked on the very first version of the pilot. When the show went to air, the producers wanted to look for someone a little closer to home – and Saltzberg was called up. He went in to meet the producers and the writing team, and quickly established that he was the man for the job. Now, he is in constant contact with the writers in order to check scripts, the actors to explain any difficult concepts he slipped in, and with the set decorators and costume designers to make sure everything is scientifically accurate. Chuck Lorre and Bill Prady have both insisted on the scientific accuracy of the show: 'We made it a point, [co-creator] Bill [Prady] and I, since the pilot to get the science right. So we're not guessing. And he'll tell us, you know. We shoot the show live in front of an audience. While we're shooting we may change a line in front of the audience. If we change a line and we're tampering with the science, some of the dialogue... we are told by David Saltzberg, our astrophysicist, that, "No, no, no, that's not correct anymore." And we change the line so that he's happy. We don't want to get a bad grade.' (For the record, Professor Saltzberg said he would give Chuck and Bill a 'B' grade for the science in *Big Bang Theory* – that's not too bad!)

Because Professor Saltzberg gets a lot of freedom to pick and choose the subjects on the show (as long as they're scientifically accurate and fit in with the general theme of the show, it's fine!), he sometimes takes the opportunity to bring important discoveries to the general public: 'It functions like a news outlet in some sense. It's also sort of a knowing wink to other physicists watching the show. I've put in references to the CERN super-collider and to recent discoveries relating to dark matter. About 90% of the matter of the universe is dark matter, so if we can get people to Google dark matter, we have the potential of millions of people learning about what 90% of the universe is.' Also, for Saltzberg, the weirder he can make it, the better: 'I go for stuff that sounds really fake – that you think is Hollywood science but find out not only is it real, it's topical,' he told *Science* magazine. In a way, his writing for *The Big Bang Theory* is a public service! And certainly a lot more fun than any science class…

One thing he doesn't get much opportunity to try is comedy-writing. Try as he might, even after being involved with many episodes, Professor Saltzberg has only successfully pitched one joke that has made it into the show itself. But he understands where the writers are coming from, and is happy to leave the jokes to the experts: 'I learned very quickly that if I try to pitch jokes, it's a bit like when I meet a random person at a party who tries to pitch some physics idea at me. These writers are pros, at the top of their field,' he told *UCLA Today*.

Professor Saltzberg writes a fascinating blog on the science of *The Big Bang Theory* called 'The Big Blog Theory'. Check it out at http://thebigblogtheory.wordpress.com/

Schrödinger's Cat

Schrödinger's Cat is one of the key experiments of quantum physics. The experiment is named for Austrian physicist Erwin Schrödinger, who devised it in 1935 (although it is definitely worth pointing out that it was simply a 'thought' experiment, and was never actually carried out by Schrödinger). Schrödinger sought to demonstrate one of the key paradoxes behind quantum physics: at the time, physicists believed that on a quantum level (extremely tiny atomic particles of matter), the same matter (such as an electron) could exist in more than one state at one time. This was called superposition. However, no scientists believed that larger matter (like a cat) could exist in more than one state. Schrödinger thought that the two beliefs could not exist together: and Schrödinger's cat is the example he used to prove it.

The experiment was to place a cat in a box (to hide it from the observer) along with a radioactive particle, a Geiger counter (which measures radioactivity) and a bottle of cyanide. The radioactive particle has an exactly 50/50 chance of breaking down over the course of an hour. If the particle did break down, the Geiger counter would go off and the bottle of cyanide released, thereby killing the cat. If not, the cat would be alive. Hence, during that hour, the cat would be both alive and dead at the same time (not either alive or dead, but actually existing in both states) to the observer who could not see the outcome – hence, superposition.

Of course, when Penny goes to Sheldon for advice about dating Leonard, she doesn't expect to be given a long spiel on one of the most difficult-to-grasp concepts in physics. But then, maybe she should've done – it is Sheldon, after all!

SCIENCE TO COME

It has to be one of the most unusual script directions in the business: 'SCIENCE TO COME'. But it appears in almost every single script written for *The Big Bang Theory*, which gets sent to Professor David Saltzberg every week. He scans the scripts for dialogue with those three key words and then he has the challenge of finding an appropriate and scientifically accurate experiment or term to fill in the blank.

Professor Saltzberg gave an example to *UCLA Today*, which came from the episode 'The Friendship Algorithm' (Season 2, Episode 13): 'So I heard about your latest [science to come] experiment – 20,000 trials and no significant results.'

Saltzberg read the rest of the script and got a sense of what kind of experiment it would need to be, and also took into account which character was speaking – in this case, it was Barry Kripke, a rival scientist at Caltech, making a snide remark about one of Leonard's experiment. That meant that the experiment had to be something related to Leonard's field of work. He also analysed the science-related dialogue surrounding the 'science to come' parentheses, such as the way the word 'trial' was used. He felt that 'trial' was wrong for the characters: 'I gave them some science, using a real experiment. Also, physicists don't really use the word "trials" that way. Little things like that can sound jarring to a physicist, although no one else cares. It's amazing – and a tribute to the writers – how much they just want to get it right. So in the final draft, it became, "I heard about your latest anti-proton decay experiment – 20,000 data runs and no significant results."'

Yet even though the writers take the science very seriously, they don't want it to disrupt the flow of the show – or to confuse the fact that this is a comedy first, not a science show. 'It's a balancing act. There has to be science but there has to be comedy. You don't get the science, you'll still get the comedy,' said Chuck Lorre. Bill Prady gave a good example of what they were trying to emulate to *Collider* magazine: 'In the earlier days, we likened it to the *I Love Lucy* moment where Ricky would rant in Cuban-Spanish and it didn't affect your ability to watch the show.'

No one can accuse *The Big Bang Theory* from not doing the science well, however, and that's begotten them some reviews from some pretty strange places. 'We had a review in *Science*, and it was a favorable review. And I thought, "Well, that's awesome". And there was something online from *The Journal of Particle Physics*,' said

Bill Prady, clearly impressed. In the *Science* review, it was even made clear that the science didn't only come from Professor Saltzberg, but that a lot of the writers knew their stuff too. The episode where Sheldon dresses up as the Doppler Effect, for example, came from the real-life Hallowe'en costume of one of the writers (the guests at his Hallowe'en party also didn't get it!)

And sometimes, the science in the story runs scarily close to real life! In Season 2, Episode 22, 'The Classified Materials Turbulence', *The Big Bang Theory* writers devised a situation for Howard Wolowitz where he realised that his design for the International Space Station toilet is faulty – and that it was going to fail in space with dire results! He attempts to devise a solution in Sheldon and Leonard's living room, employing all their brain power. 'About 2–3 weeks after the episode aired, the toilet on the International Space Station did fail and it failed almost exactly as we predicted it might,' said Bill Prady to the NASA team who were visiting the set. 'I was kind of happy about this because we looked at the schematics for the toilet, and we said, "Where is this thing weak?" so we could come up with what Wolowitz thinks might go wrong. We pinpointed what looked like a weakness and in fact that's how the toilet actually failed! The moral of the story is, if you're installing plumbing off the planet Earth, consult comedy writers!'

Still, even when he is accurate to the point of prescience, there are still people who complain, as Professor Saltzberg has learned: 'If I look on the [Internet] message boards, there's still complaints – no matter how right you get the science, there's going to be some fraction of people who think it's wrong!' There's just no pleasing some fans!

Selective Mutism

In *The Big Bang Theory*, Rajesh Koothrappali suffers from selective mutism when it comes to talking to women. Even in the presence of woman he has known for a long time, such as Penny, Raj cannot overcome his fear and talk to her. His only cure for his mutism is alcohol, which lowers his inhibitions enough to enable him to talk to women. In fact, the only woman he seems to be able to talk to not under the influence of alcohol is his mum!

Selective mutism is a rare but well-documented communication disorder, especially prevalent among children. It is normally accompanied by severe shyness or other social anxiety. There is no 'cure' as such, but through therapy and treatments specified to the individual, it can be improved.

There are signs that Raj might be able to overcome his inability to talk to women however, as in 'The Terminator Decoupling' (Season 2, Episode 17) we see that alcohol has as much a placebo effect as anything else – as he can talk to *Terminator: The Sarah Connor Chronicles* actress Summer Glau 'under the influence' of non-alcoholic beer. When Howard points out to him that it is non-alcoholic, Raj clams up again.

Sitcoms

The multi-camera sitcom is dead! At least, that was the general cry from critics and audiences alike after the end of *Friends* and *Everybody Loves Raymond*. The multi-camera sitcom is a comedy show filmed predominantly on a studio set in front of a live audience, with four or more cameras shooting the action. It enables shows to be filmed faster and with fewer takes, but doesn't easily allow for many tightly edited sequences, multiple locations or visual effects as a single-camera sitcom might. The multi-camera format dominated the shows of the 1970s and 80s. By contrast, single-camera sitcoms – which have no live audience – made a dramatic revival in the 2000s, with shows like *Scrubs*, *The Office* and *30 Rock*, and many television producers (and the networks they worked for) saw the multi-camera set-up as old-fashioned. 'Our first season, the talk was that the multi-camera sitcom was dead,' said Jim Parsons to *New York Magazine*. 'But to me, the live aspect is rooted in theater; it's too ingrained in our DNA to ever fully go away.' The success of *The Big Bang Theory* just goes to prove Jim right – it hasn't stopped them from doing well, and that doesn't look likely to change in the future.

Smoot, George and Other Scientific Inspiration

George Smoot is an astrophysicist who won the Nobel Prize in Physics in 2006, for his work measuring cosmic microwave backgrounds with the Cosmic Background Explorer Satellite – work that helped to further the Big Bang Theory of the universe. Smoot was therefore enchanted by the *Big Bang Theory* sitcom, which seemed essentially dedicated to his field, and quickly became a fan. Before the second season started, he wrote to the creators Chuck Lorre and Bill Prady to find out whether he could get involved in an appearance on the show. 'I think it's a great opportunity, and it's about the Big Bang which is what my life's work is about,' said Smoot. The creators leapt at the chance to increase their scientific kudos by having a real Nobel Prize winner on board, and found a creative way to write him into an episode.

He appeared at the end of Season 2, in Episode 13, 'The Terminator Decoupling'. Sheldon and the gang take a special trip to meet George Smoot so that Sheldon could request that they co-write a paper together, an offer which George categorically refuses! George thought the script was hilarious, and absolutely loved his time on set (he found the acting part much more difficult than he imagined, even though he was only playing himself!). He hung out with the cast, correcting Jim's pronunciation of certain physics terms and generally imbuing *The Big Bang Theory* set with some authentic physics cred. 'He's bigger than Britney Spears,' said Kunal, referring to George Smoot's celebrity status amongst physicists. As an added bonus in the episode, Leonard was reading *Wrinkles in Time* by George Smoot on the train, one of those key realistic details that the writers never miss out on, as it makes total sense that Leonard would be catching up on his Smoot-related knowledge before meeting him!

The Big Bang Theory hasn't been Smoot's only

appearance in front of a camera either. After his cameo appearance on the hit sitcom, he went on to win the one million dollar grand prize on the TV game show *Are You Smarter than a 5th Grader?* (the U.S. version of *Are You Smarter than a Ten Year Old?*). On the show, he took the time to explain what his Nobel Prize winning research was all about (and he did it in a much more concise way than Sheldon ever could!): 'We figured out over the years a way to make a picture of the embryo universe…So it's the very beginning of the universe, but it's got the blueprint for what's gonna happen later.' He sailed through the answers to the questions in all categories, but once he realised that his encyclopedic knowledge wasn't making for very good TV, he took a gamble and decided to 'copy' the answers of one of the fifth graders. Luckily, she got it right, and he still went on to win the million – one of only two people ever to do so. His final question was: 'What U.S. state is home to Acadia National Park?' He answered correctly: 'Maine'.

In George's wake, several other physicists have appeared on the show, from Hayden Planetarium astrophysicist Neil de Grasse Tyson and Columbia University professor Brian Greene. It's pretty surreal for Bill Prady and Chuck Lorre, who had to do quite a lot of in-depth research to basically 'become' physicists before they could write about them: 'When Chuck Lorre and I first started working on *The Big Bang Theory*, we had to figure out how to quickly become physicists and one of the books we picked up was *The Elegant Universe* by Brian Greene.' In fact, it ended up being a bit of a PR stunt for Brian Greene, who was on a promotional tour with his new book *The Hidden Reality*, which had just been published. In an episode, Brian Greene is gently mocked by Sheldon for trying to talk to 'ordinary people' about science (an impossible task, in Sheldon's view), which earned him a bit of Hollywood sheen to put on his CV alongside his physics accomplishments! It's a fair warning to other scientists who might be keen on appearing in the show: you become fair game for getting laughed at! Maybe one day arguably the most famous scientist in the world, Stephen Hawking, will appear on the show, but if he does, he had better bring his sense of humour!

Unfortunately, having a world class scientist on the show is much more exciting for the producers than the media. Johnny Galecki told Bullz-Eye.com: 'we were very excited to have George Smoot on. And [Chuck Lorre] would tell the press conferences, "Oh, we have George Smoot on." It was like the big teaser, where he would see 100 blank faces staring back at him. "You know, George Smoot. Nobel Prize winner George Smoot." Blank expression. "And we also have Summer Glau." "Oh, Summer Glau!" And the pencils start whirring.' The media obviously need to catch up – having a Nobel Prize winner on board is a big deal!

Soft Kitty

'Soft Kitty' is Sheldon's favourite lullaby, sung to him when he is sick by his mother or by Penny if his mother isn't around. The little melody has attracted its own kind of cult following, with the lyrics appearing on T-shirts and on other merchandise. But how did 'Soft Kitty' come about? It turned out that Bill Prady had heard someone singing it at his daughter's preschool, and he was inspired to include it in the show – it was exactly the kind of inane tune that would be hilarious associated with Sheldon.

It proved so popular that CBS.com decided to run a contest around it. Launched on 6 January 2011, CBS.com encouraged fans to upload a 30-second video of themselves singing 'Soft Kitty'. The prize would be a trip to Los Angeles to watch a live taping of *The Big*

Bang Theory. Jeff Clark, the Vice President of CBS.com, described it in their press release as: '*The Big Bang Theory* continues to grow in popularity both on television and online. Through this contest, we wanted to find a creative way to discover the show's most passionate fans and encourage them to compete with each other for the ultimate prize for any *The Big Bang Theory* fanatic.' The winner was username 'amahacek', who filmed a hilarious version of the song featuring a robot, equations and a very robotic voice.

Stuart

Stuart is the owner of the Comic Center, where the guys go to fulfill all their comic book related desires (including meeting Stan Lee). He is an artist too, who attended Rhode Island School of Design.

Sheldon is jealous of him because he gets 45% off comic books. He is played by Kevin Sussman.

Sussman, Kevin

Kevin Sussman plays Stuart (see above). He was born 4 December 1970 on Staten Island, New York and got his start in the acting world whilst studying under

KEVIN SUSSMAN, WHO PLAYS STUART

renowned acting coach Uta Hagen for four years (she has also taught Sigourney Weaver, Whoopi Goldberg and Al Pacino, amongst many others). He is best known for his recurring role as Walter in *Ugly Betty*. He is great friends with John Ross Bowie, who plays Barry Kripke on *The Big Bang Theory*. Interestingly, Bill Prady tweeted that Kevin was one of the finalists to play the role of Howard Wolowitz, which eventually went to Simon Helberg.

Syndication Record

In May 2010, a bidding war raged through Hollywood with all the big-name U.S. networks taking part: Fox, Tribune, FX, TBS and MTV. The property at auction? Syndication rights for *The Big Bang Theory*. Syndication refers to the rights to play an episode after it has already aired once on network television (so repeat or rerun episodes). Sitcoms are a popular choice for syndication as they don't necessarily need to be aired in order. According to Deadline magazine, the auction was won by TBS, who paid $1.5 million per episode for cable rights, and by Fox who won broadcast station rights for $500,000 per episode.

The total $2 million deal for *The Big Bang Theory*

makes it a syndication record for any show. It beat CBS and Chuck Lorre's other successful sitcom *Two and a Half Men*, which sold for $800,000 per episode and even beat out the popular sitcom *Seinfeld*, which went for $1 million per episode.

T

Theorists, The

Is imitation the sincerest form of flattery? That might be the cliché, but when it happened to *The Big Bang Theory*, executive producer and co-creator Chuck Lorre was less than impressed.

The first mention of *The Theorists* came in one of Chuck's infamous vanity cards. Vanity card #277, which aired following *The Big Bang Theory* episode on 8 February 2010, read: '…Belarus does have a bustling TV production industry. One of their most recent hits is a sitcom about four nerdy scientists who live next door to a beautiful blonde waitress. The characters are named Sheldon, Leo, Howard, Raj and Natasha, and the show is entitled *The Theorists*…each episode appears to be a Russian translation of a *Big Bang Theory* episode.' It was clear that Chuck was very unhappy with this development, and wanted the entire world to know about it.

Unfortunately for Chuck, when he tried to get the Warner Brothers legal team to take the show off the air, he encountered a hitch with the Belarussian bureaucratic system: the TV production studio who made *The Theorists* were closely tied to the Belarus government, and therefore any attempt to force through a copyright violation notice would be bogged down in a bureaucratic quagmire.

In the end, the actors in the Belarus show decided to plead ignorance of the existence of *The Big Bang Theory*. But then the actor who played the 'alternate Leonard', Dmitriy Tankovich, told Russian website Charter 97: 'I'm upset. At first the actors were told all legal issues were resolved. We didn't know it wasn't the case, so when the creators of *The Big Bang Theory* started talking about the show, I was embarrassed. I can't understand why our people first do, and then think. I consider this to be the rock bottom of my

career. And I don't want to take part in a stolen show.'
The Theorists was promptly cancelled.

Twitter

It's not surprising that such a modern show as *Big Bang*
is fully up to date on Twitter, but funnily enough, its
two main stars, Johnny Galecki and Jim Parsons, are
Twitter-free, for the moment. For all the rest of your
up-to-the-minute *The Big Bang Theory* news, here are
the accounts to follow:

Bill Prady (co-creator/executive producer) @billprady
Kaley Cuoco (Penny) @KaleyCuoco
Simon Helberg (Howard Wolowitz) @simonhelberg
Kunal Nayyar (Raj Koothrappali) @kunalnayyar
Mayim Bialik (Amy Farrah Fowler) @missmayim
Wil Wheaton (as himself) @wilw
John Ross Bowie (Barry Kripke) @JohnRossBowie
Steven Molaro (writer) @SteveMolaro
Dave Goetsch (writer) @goetech

United Kingdom

Channel 4 is the home of *The Big Bang Theory* in the UK. It secured the rights to air the show on Channel 4 and its sister channel E4 in September 2007, after a bidding war amongst UK television stations. The UK critics were much more open to the show that their US counterparts, and many of them compared the show favourably with similar-themed UK shows like *The IT Crowd* and *Clone*. The *Mirror* wrote of *The Big Bang Theory*: 'If you think that sounds suspiciously like another Channel 4 comedy, *The IT Crowd* which will also return on Friday, then you'd be bang on – except that *The Big Bang Theory* is funnier, cleverer and American…Landing in the same week that BBC Three foisted its own astonishingly abysmal new science sitcom *Clone* on us (so bad it hurt your eyes to look at it) I can't recommend this enough.' The *Guardian* also noted the comparisons to *IT Crowd*: 'There are echoes of Graham Linehan's *The IT Crowd* in the social incomprehension of its male leads, but it is played at a slicker pitch.' Some reviews, like that of the *Independent*, were less favourable: 'There are some OK gags buried beneath the over-emphatic laugh track. But most of them rely on our two heroes switching, when it suits the writers, from tongue-tied geeks to knowing and worldly gagmeisters.' Still, after the first episode aired on Channel 4 on Valentine's Day 2008, the show garnered a very respectable 1,000,000 viewers, and continued to pull in similar figures for its first season.

Despite such good ratings, *The Big Bang Theory* flew most under the radar on UK television screens. But once the show and its stars started winning big awards in the US (such as Jim Parsons' Emmy), it started to pick up steam. As the *Metro* said: 'now that Jim Parsons has deservedly landed an Emmy for his portrayal of the über-nerdy and other-worldly Sheldon, more people will sit up and take notice.' That proved to be true, and for Episode 13 1.3 million people tuned in – the show's most-watched episode yet.

Two years later, and Season 4 aired on 4 November 2010. The show then became the most-watched programme per week for E4, proving that the UK's hunger for geeks was still going strong!

Vanity Cards

One of Chuck Lorre's signature quirks is his vanity
cards. A vanity card is a traditionally a snapshot of the
production company's logo and is only shown for a
second (or sometimes even less) at the very end of a
show. Chuck's original vanity card, for shows such as
Cybill and *Grace Under Fire*, was an example of this –
with his company name ('Chuck Lorre Productions')
shown on the screen of an old Apple Macintosh SE
computer, itself sitting on a messy wooden writer's
desk. But Chuck Lorre has since turned the vanity card

into its own art form, producing a mini-essay once a week on all subjects ranging from his childhood and current affairs to griping about the stars of his shows.

It started on 24 September 1997, when the pilot episode of Chuck's new show *Dharma & Greg* aired for the first time. He thanked fans for 'freeze-framing' on his vanity card – back in the Nineties, the only way anyone would get to read them was if they had recorded his show on their VCRs and pressed 'pause' at the exact right moment. The reward for their efforts was a mini-essay by Chuck on his personal beliefs. It's a tradition that has continued throughout Chuck's career, after every episode from *Dharma & Greg*, *Two and a Half Men*, *The Big Bang Theory* and *Mike & Molly*.

The vanity cards have been a fun indulgence for Chuck, who has created his own little inside-joke in the industry. But sometimes the jokes turn sour, and the vanity cards turn against him. His cards have been censored many times by the network, but he finds a way to get around the censorship by posting the original versions on his personal website. He also got into big trouble with Charlie Sheen, during the rows surrounding *Two and a Half Men*: 'Chuck Lorre really fired the first shot with those vanity cards,' said an anonymous television producer to *Fox News*. In several

Chuck Lorre, who is famous for his 'vanity cards', celebrates his Hollywood Walk of Fame star

of his vanity cards, Chuck had written less-than-pleasant diatribes against Charlie Sheen, although often omitting Sheen's name. The gloves came off, however, when the episode of *Two and a Half Men* that aired on Valentine's Day 2011 featured a vanity card reading: 'If Charlie Sheen outlives me, I'm gonna be really pissed' (Vanity Card #329). Following Chuck's mini-rant, the relationship between producer and star got increasingly out of hand. The anonymous television producer continued to Fox: 'That's really not the place for those opinions to be aired. I can understand why Charlie Sheen would be angry about that. No one wins when you air those private battles in public.'

Eventually, Chuck Lorre agreed, and on 25 February 2011 the furore was enough to make him reconsider his vanity cards. 'It was more fun writing these things when I was fairly certain no one was reading them. That is no longer the case. These days it seems like every vanity card is getting scrutinised and criticised by network executives, corporate legal departments and publicity departments, TV journalists and tabloid bloggers,' he wrote after a *Mike & Molly* episode. His hiatus was short-lived, however, and just three days later he was up and running again, with his vanity cards continuing in fine form.

Video Games

The boys love their video games and during the episode 'The Gothowitz Deviation' (Season 3, Episode 3), we get to see just how much as Sheldon is forced to list his consoles and games to the police after their apartment is robbed. They have: a classic Nintendo, Super-Nintendo, Nintendo 64, Wii, Xbox, Xbox 359, Playstation 2 and a Playstation 3. In terms of games, the boys have a vast collection, with all three *Halo* games, *Call of Duty 1–3*, two versions of *Rock Band*, the entire *Final Fantasy* collection, *The Legend of Zelda*, *The Legend of Zelda: Ocarina of Time*, *The Legend of Zelda: Twilight Princess*, *Super Mario Brothers*, *Super Mario Galaxy*, *Mario Kart Wii*, *Mario and Sonic at the Winter Olympics* and *Pacman*.

The boys are so dedicated to their video games that one of them even has its own night: *Halo* night, normally on a Wednesday at 8pm – except for if one of the boys is on a date, which doesn't happen too often!

Wheaton, Wil

Another sci-fi legend to make an appearance on *The Big Bang Theory* is Richard William 'Wil' Wheaton, who is best known for playing Wesley Crusher in *Star Trek: The Next Generation* from 1987–1990. His character earned the dubious honour of becoming one of the most maligned characters in the *Star Trek* canon. But Wil took the hatred in stride: 'As I've gotten older and the people who watched who were around the same age as me have gotten older, I've learned that the people who were like "We hate you and here's the 67 ways we

WIL WHEATON, WHO APPEARS IN *THE BIG BANG THEORY* AS
SHELDON'S NEMESIS

want you to be impaled by a Klingon and killed" were truly a very vocal and cruel minority,' he told audiences at San Diego Comic-Con 2010.

After *Star Trek*, he became well known on the internet for his writing on his weblog, *Wil Wheaton Dot Net* (WWDN), and his blog entries were combined into a book called *Dancing Barefoot*, which he published under his own independent publishing company Monolith Press. In 2003, his blog was named 'Best Celebrity Weblog' by Forbes.com. At present, he runs the weblog Wil Wheaton Dot Net: in Exile. On his blog, he talked about his experiences with *The Big Bang Theory*: 'When [Bill Prady] first talked to me about working on the show, [he] told me that I'd be playing a "delightfully evil version" of myself. This sounded like a lot of fun to me, but it was more difficult to find that character than you'd think.'

Whiteboards

Nothing about *The Big Bang Theory* set is accidental – and that is especially true for the whiteboards that are often seen in the living room or in Sheldon's office. The man in charge of the whiteboards is on-set scientist David Saltzberg who has lots of fun in thinking up equations to put on the boards as an 'Easter Egg' for keen-eyed viewers. 'I write the equations so it doesn't look like nonsense. Often, things that the characters say they're working on will match up with what's on the whiteboard. It's just there as background, so it probably doesn't matter. But I have fun with it. I found out there are people trying to guess what's on there and why,' said Professor Saltzberg.

One of the most prominent examples is Sheldon's whiteboard in the living room. In the pilot episode, Sheldon talks about writing up a parody of the Born-Oppenheimer Approximation, which is a mathematical shortcut scientists use when solving quantum chemical equations. Professor Saltzberg actually made sure that it was a real parody ('it made our consultant laugh,' said Bill Prady to the *Washington Post*) – just showing the extra levels of depth the show goes to make sure its gags are authentic to all of its viewers – even those with a theoretical physics PhD.

Other times, David Saltzberg drops in little real-world references that are a nod to things going on outside of the show. For example, when the esteemed physicist John Wheeler died in April 2008 (he was a theoretical physicist who coined the terms 'black hole', 'quantum foam' and 'wormhole'), David Saltzberg put his most famous equations up on the whiteboards as a tribute. Once, when he knew his grad students were coming to visit, he put the solutions to an exam paper they were had taken on the boards. David Saltzberg also finds it interesting to hear about other scientists who worked as consultants for the television and movie industry. One such consultant, Martin Gundersen, who worked on the 1985 movie *Real Genius*, came onto the set. Professor Saltzberg said of Dr. Gundersen's work: 'Now that I know how much goes into getting sets and stories right, I was in awe of what a great job [he] had done, from the sets to weaving physics right into the plot line.' He then made sure that the same whiteboards featured in *Real Genius* showed up on the set of *Big Bang Theory* when Dr. Gundersen came to visit.

But most of the time, the whiteboards do relate to the show. Bill Prady told the *Journal Gazette*: 'We're working on giving Sheldon an actual problem that he's going to be working on throughout the season so there's actual progress to the boards…We work hard to get all the science right.'

Winkle, Leslie

Dr. Leslie Winkle is a PhD Experimental physicist at Caltech working on high energy physics. She is a female version of Leonard Hofstadter – incredibly smart, successful in her field and a bit socially awkward (but not so much so as Sheldon). In fact, she takes great pleasure in belittling or insulting Sheldon at any chance she gets! She is also quite sexually promiscuous, and seduces first Leonard and then Howard into purely sexual relationships.

The writers of the show attempted to turn Dr. Leslie Winkle into a main character on the show but realised that they couldn't write enough material for her. Johnny Galecki attempted to explain the situation to Bullz-Eye.com: 'We love [Sara Gilbert], and we love having her there. It's just a situation of, when is it right to bring her back? You don't want to waste an actress like Sara Gilbert. Fortunately, she doesn't need the work and would rather wait for it to be a good reason for the character to come back.'

We hope Dr. Winkle comes back soon, as it's always great to see Sheldon taken down a peg or two by her witty remarks.

Wolowitz, Howard

Howard Wolowitz, M.Eng, is the only main male character without a PhD – and Sheldon doesn't let him

HOWARD WOLOWITZ IS PLAYED BY SIMON HELBERG

forget it! He is also the character who still lives with his mom. He works at Caltech in their aerospace engineering department, and is always working on projects for NASA or the International Space Station.

Whereas his best friend Raj cannot speak to women at all under normal circumstances, Howard considers himself something of a Casanova. 'You might say he's the most delusional of the bunch,' laughs Simon Helberg, who plays Howard on the show. 'He definitely thinks he's god's gift to women and he's overly confident and he's sort of like a James Bond, but he's ready at any situation, any place, any language, any time to land the girl and that's sort of his whole outlook on life revolves around women and getting them any way he can, so.' Somehow though, even despite himself Howard has managed to land himself a beautiful girlfriend named Bernadette. In Season 4, Episode 20, 'The Herb Garden Germination', Howard proposes to her, which she accepts despite her reservations.

Howard is based on a real life person that Bill Prady knew. He told the audience at PaleyFest: 'There was a guy named Dave and Dave had a series of women, all kinds of women. And said he had two rules and the rules were: proposition every woman, have no standards.' That sums up Howard pretty well!

World of Warcraft (and other MMORPGs)

Several episodes of *The Big Bang Theory* feature the boys (and sometimes even Penny) playing MMORPGs (Massively Multiplayer Online Role Playing Games). *World of Warcraft* (WoW) is the most popular MMORPG in the world, with over 12 million subscribers. *WoW* takes place in the fantasy realm of Azeroth, and subscribers choose an avatar (or toon) which they use to explore the world, go on quests and interact with other characters.

One episode of *The Big Bang Theory*, 'The Zarnecki Incursion' (Season 4, Episode 19) highlighted just how serious a MMORPG can get. Dedicated players, like Sheldon, can spend thousands of man hours building up their avatar's attributes (in Sheldon's case, he had built up the blood elf Sheldor to level 85) and they can collect rare items that can be worth 'real world' value. Therefore, when Sheldor's account is hacked and his character and items stolen, he is so devastated that he calls the police! The police can't do anything for him, and so Sheldon and the boys decided to go on a real-life quest to find the culprit and get back Sheldon's account. When they fail, Penny shows up just in time to dish out a Nebraska-style quest (she beats him up!)

Penny is in a good place to understand Sheldon's pain, as she once got addicted to a MMORPG when Sheldon introduced her to *Age of Conan* in 'The Barbarian Sublimation' (Season 2, Episode 3). It soon took over her life, however, and she has to stay away from online games now lest she forgets about the real world completely!

Writers' Strike

On 5 November, 2007, over 12,000 film, television and radio writers belonging to the Writer's Guild of America went on strike, bringing Hollywood to a halt. The strike was over compensation for writers, who felt that in proportion to the huge profits the hit studios made, their share was not enough. For a new show like *The Big Bang Theory*, whose first season had only just begun in September 2007, it was a massive blow. 'It absolutely hurt us,' recalled Chuck Lorre. 'The show was building momentum. It was on eight weeks before the strike started. I think we aired eight episodes and each episode kind of was going up just a little bit in the ratings so it was building. Slowly, but it was building, and it was really exciting because you could see it…and it all stopped and it was horrible. There was crying. I mean…there was crying.'

MEMBERS OF THE *BIG BANG THEORY* CAST SHOW THEIR SUPPORT FOR THE WRITERS' STRIKE OF 2007/8

It was especially disruptive as the strike was called right in the middle of filming an episode. The cast and crew had to walk off the set, unsure of the show's future. They were devastated, but they weren't prepared to give up. If anything, the forced break from the show made them realise just what they were missing, and how much they had grown to love working together.

As soon as the strike ended on 12 February 2008, they got back to work. 'We were the first show to go back into production,' said Johnny Galecki to Bullz-Eye.com. 'We were all just gnawing at the bit to do so. I think we realised that we love it there and we love working together. If we were only putting 99% in to it before the Writers' Strike, I think definitely everyone was putting 100% into it afterwards.'

Kaley Cuoco echoed Johnny's thoughts: 'It went from zero to sixty in 0.2 seconds here [laughs] as soon as the strike ended, but we were ecstatic to get back… At the same time, it kind of feels like not a day passed either. We had to walk in the middle of the episode that we were filming when the strike hit and we came back and jumped right back into that same episode and finished up and it felt great.' It also meant that the show didn't have to go up against ratings heavyweight *Dancing with the Stars*, which had chosen not to return for the rest of the season after the strikes.

In the end, where other shows faltered because of the Writers' Strike, *The Big Bang Theory* came back stronger than ever – albeit a bit shorter than originally planned. The first season had only 17 episodes, whereas the following two seasons had 23. What doesn't kill you makes you stronger!

X-Men and other comics

Comic book night – which happens every Wednesday – is one of the most important nights of the week for the *Big Bang* gang. The comic book store is a place of refuge for them, where they go to escape from it all. At the comic store they fight over the new issues and resolve heated comic-related debates. One such debate was between Sheldon and Howard in Season 3, Episode 2, 'The Jiminy Conjecture', who had a bet as to whether Wolverine from *X-Men* was born with bone claws. Sheldon won the argument (of course) by pulling out the *Origins* issue which proves him right.

In the show, the store is called simply 'Comic Center' and it is built entirely on set. It even has its own website which you can visit: www.thecomiccenter.com. Wil Wheaton (who appears as a fictional version of himself in a few episodes) wrote on his blog: 'The comic book shop set is incredible, and the attention to detail is unbelievable. Because *BBT* is produced at Warners, and Warners is affiliated with DC, they have tons of DC books (including archival editions that I wanted to, uh, borrow, like you wouldn't believe), tons of sculpted minis and action figures, and posters all over the shop that are actually part of current storylines in comics. Their set dressing people change those posters and stuff to reflect what's happening in the DCU [DC Universe], which I thought was awesome.'

Some fans have noticed that there is a tendency on the show to favour DC Comics over Marvel Comics. For all those non-comic-geeks out there, DC and Marvel are rival publishers and between them they own some of the most well-known characters in comics. DC own *Batman*, *Superman* and *Wonder Woman*, among others, while Marvel is home to *X-Men*, *Spiderman*, the *Fantastic Four* and many more.

Bill Prady took some time out at Comic-Con to explain why the show sometimes seemed to express a preference for one side over the other. One reason was simple logistics, which Wil Wheaton referred to: DC Comics are owned by Warner Brothers, who produce *The Big Bang Theory*. It is therefore much easier to clear the rights to show a DC comic on air, than it is for a Marvel. Also complicating matters is the writers' personal preferences: 'I'm a DC comics guy,' said Bill, 'and my big argument on the staff is with Steve Molaro, co-executive producer, who's a big Marvel comics guy. And then I won, because I outrank him. But we're doing a lot more Marvel stuff. We were writing a long-running dialogue about Wolverine and whether or not he was born with bone claws. I was just talking with Len Wein (creator of Wolverine) and he was, so I got it right.'

Yet both Bill and Chuck Lorre are very careful about keeping the references organic. They know their audience, who wouldn't take very well to having their favourite show marred by product placement, even if it is comic-book related. CBS once 'suggested' to Chuck Lorre that they include more references to the movie *X-Men Origins: Wolverine* in *The Big Bang Theory* order to promote the film. Chuck refused – and ultimately, Chuck gets the final say.

Also, Warner Brothers' association with DC Comics

doesn't prevent Chuck and Bill from working with some Marvel greats, as demonstrated when Stan Lee made a guest appearance on their show. Stan Lee and Chuck Lorre had worked together at Marvel Animations and to this day have mutual respect and admiration for each other's work. In fact, Stan told *Access Hollywood* that *The Big Bang Theory* was his favourite show on TV at the moment, and that he didn't need much convincing to make an appearance. 'To me it's one of the cleverest shows in the world… And they keep mentioning my name on the show, which is great!'

Y

YouTube

YouTube has played an important role in *The Big Bang Theory*'s history. It was on YouTube that Chuck Lorre and Bill Prady found the now-famous music video to the Barenaked Ladies' theme song 'The History of Everything'. Chuck Lorre explained to *Television Without Pity*: 'We were going to shoot a video for the song this summer and we found this thing on YouTube. This guy is a student in London and he did it as part of a school project. And we just all agreed we can't do any better than this. It's phenomenal. So that's our video. And I think he got a good grade.'

The student was called Mark Burbery, and he had the idea to do a continuous line drawing of each lyric in the show's theme song. He bought a huge roll of wallpaper and shot the whole thing as one long video, which was then sped up to match the speed of the song. When he was asked by Chuck and Bill to replicate the video officially for CBS, Mark had to change a couple of things from his original. For one, it turned out that he had misheard one of the lyrics (easy to do when a singer sings as fast as Ed Robertson) and put a drawing of the encyclopedia *Encarta* instead of the philosopher 'Descartes'. They also had him draw in the title card (the five *Big Bang Theory* cast members jumping in the air) at the end of the video, instead of his spray-painted BANG! If you do a YouTube search for '*The Big Bang Theory*: Drawing', you will be able to find the official video as hosted by CBS.

Zero Zero Zero Zero

Is there anywhere more sacred than Sheldon's spot on the sofa? After much trial and error, Sheldon decided on the sole place in the living room where he is comfortable sitting. Everything about the spot is perfect: the ambient temperature, the cross-breeze, the angle to the television and the ability to chat to the other seated spots in the room. It is Sheldon's cherished place in the room. Others sit there on pain of death! (Or at least, on pain of Sheldon's death-glare, which is normally enough to get them moving!)

In Season 2, Episode 16, 'The Cushion Saturation', Sheldon says that if he were to plot his life as a function on a four-dimensionsal Cartesian coordinate system, then the moment in time, that he chose to sit on that specific spot on the sofa, would be zero–zero–zero–zero. A four-dimensional Catersian coordinate system envisages three dimensions of space (up–down, left–right, and forward–backward, normally plotted on a graph as x, y and z) and one dimension of time. For Sheldon, the point at which all these lines meet is the sofa: it is his one constant, and in the world of *Big Bang Theory*, it's one thing that we hope will never change.